Table of Contents

To Parents and Teachers

Just as Jesus used parables to teach His followers Christian values, you too, can use concrete objects to relate difficult concepts to your students. To make learning easier, the author has chosen familiar and interesting objects such as a pitcher of water, a pencil and eraser, and a football helmet. These common and easily located objects will make learning about difficult concepts such as God's love, forgiveness, and the armor of God easier and more enjoyable. Lessons include "Warning Signs," "Behavior Thermometer," and "Speed Limit" plus many more.

Each lesson can easily be adapted to any learning setting: Sunday School, Christian classroom, Vacation Bible School, camp, or home story-time. The amount of delivery time will vary depending on group discussion time, etc. If you have been wondering how to highlight Bible themes and teach Christian concepts, *Five-Minute Bible Object Lessons* is for you. For ages 5-10.

Five-Minute Bible Object Lessons

by
Clifford Chalmers Cain

illustrated by Ted Warren

Cover by Ted Warren

Shining Star Publications, Copyright © 1992

A Division of Good Apple

ISBN No. 0-86653-694-9

Shining Star Publications
A Division of Good Apple
1204 Buchanan St., Box 299
Carthage, IL 62321-0299

Unless otherwise indicated, the New International Version of the Bible was used in preparing the activities in this book.

Dedication

This book is lovingly dedicated to Rachel Mariël and Zachary Matheüs–daughter and son, heirs of the covenant, recipients of God's grace, and sources of both great joy and gray hair.

SS2824

The Bad Along with the Good

Props: A bowl of popcorn, containing both popped and unpopped kernels

I have a bowl filled with something which I am sure you will recognize and perhaps want to eat! What do I have here? (Invite the children to respond.) You're right: it is a bowl filled with popcorn. How many of you enjoy eating popcorn? (Invite a show of hands.) I enjoy popcorn, too.

Let's look in the bowl and see what delicious-looking kernels of popcorn we can find. (Do so.) Umm, look at this one (hold it up) and this one (hold it up). I bet this whole bowl contains nothing but good-tasting, popped kernels of popcorn. (Continue investigating.)

Ugh, what's this? (Hold up an unpopped kernel.) And this? (Hold up another unpopped kernel.) I'm not sure I would like to eat this kernel: it's not popped; it doesn't look very delicious; it probably would taste very bad. I guess this bowl has good and bad kernels of popcorn in it.

Girls and boys, the world we live in has good and bad in it. Some people have enough to eat; some people do not. Some people treat others well; some do not. Some people are healthy; some are not. Some people are willing to share; some are not. Some people want to live peacefully; some do not.

I'm certain that the good things in the world make God happy, and I'm sure that the bad things in the world make God sad. He does not want people to starve. He does not want people to be mistreated. He does not want people to be sick. He does not want people to be selfish. He does not want war. Since God loves all people, He wants good things for everyone.

God knows that there is bad along with the good in the world, but He doesn't like it! God wants you and me to join with Him and with others to overcome bad with good and make the world a better place.

Prayer:

> God, who loves everyone, we thank you that you work for good. We know that you would like the world to be a better place. Help all of us to join with you so that bad may be replaced with good. In Jesus' name. Amen.

 SS2824

Plugging into the Power

Props: A small electric typewriter and a portable desk upon which to place it

Boys and girls, I was just going to type an important letter to someone. I hope you won't mind if I finish it now. Now let me see; where was I in that letter? (Begin using the typewriter, which has not been plugged in.) What's the matter? Something has happened to the typewriter! Girls and boys, why is this typewriter not working? (Encourage answers from the children.)

Oh, yes. I see the typewriter is not plugged in so it is not receiving any electrical power. No wonder it won't work correctly! Without being plugged into the power, it won't do what it is supposed to do.

Boys and girls, all of us have a tremendous responsibility as Christians: we are to remember to follow Jesus and obey God's rules in the Bible, be kind to people, look after others as well as after ourselves, and try to understand people rather than pass judgment on them.

Unless we are plugged into the power of God, we will never be able to do this well. Without receiving strength, encouragement, and consolation from God, we won't be the kind of Christian people we should be, and we won't be able to do the things we are supposed to do.

How do we plug into God's power? We give our lives to Jesus. Then we go to church, share in worship, attend Sunday School, ask God in our prayers to help us, follow the example of other Christians, and try as hard as we can to do what God wants us to do.

Without being plugged into the power, the typewriter would not do what it was supposed to do. If we are not plugged into the power of God, we will not be able to do what we are supposed to do!

Prayer:

Powerful Father, we give you thanks that you care about us and that you are devoted to helping us be the best that we can be. Forgive us for the times that we have failed you, and encourage us to try harder. In the name of Jesus. Amen.

Knowing the Father

Prop: A picture of a father, preferably the storyteller's

I have a special picture with me. (Hold up the picture so the children can see it.) Do you know who this is? (Let children share their ideas.)

The man in this picture is my father. Let me tell you about him. (The storyteller should tell about his own father.) He was born in 1886 and was near retirement when I was born. Earlier in his life, he drove an army supply truck in the first World War in France. He was also a baseball player, a chauffeur, a commercial truck driver, and a fireman. He was born in western Pennsylvania and married my mother over forty years ago. He died when I was a little boy. One of the fondest memories I have of my father is his walking with me in the backyard and holding my hand.

You now know quite a bit about my father, and you learned it from me, his son. By my talking about him, I have told you about him. In sharing about my father, I have revealed him to you even though you have never met him.

In Matthew 11:27b, Jesus said, . . . "no one knows the Father except the Son and those to whom the Son chooses to reveal him."

Through Jesus, through His words and actions, we learn about God. We know that God is love, that God forgives us as we forgive each other, that God does not remember our sins but separates us from our sins as far as the east is from the west, that God loved the world so much that He gave His only Son, and that whoever believes in Him shall not perish but have eternal life.

Jesus, God's Son, tells us and shows us about God. "No one knows the Father except the Son and those to whom the Son chooses to reveal him." Jesus knows His heavenly Father, and He has chosen to reveal Him to us. Let's praise God for being the kind of God He is, and let's thank Jesus for making God known to us.

Prayer:

> Magnificent and merciful God, thank you for sending Jesus to tell us all about you. In Him we see a reflection of your love, your grace, your redemption, and your patience. Knowing you, we can respond to your love by our being loving, to your grace by our being gracious, to your redemption by learning that the best things in life are *given,* not earned, and to your patience by our being patient. We pray in Jesus' name. Amen.

SS2824

Found or Given? A Perspective of Vision

Props: Two five-dollar bills and a birthday card

I want to tell you about some money I have with me. Here's one five-dollar bill, and here is another. (Show the children the two bills.) Each bill is worth five-dollars, but they do not have the same value to me.

I found the first five-dollar bill while jogging. Perhaps someone lost it; maybe it fell out of someone's pocket. I'm not sure what I'll do with it; perhaps I'll buy something.

I received the other five-dollar bill in this card. (Show the children the card.) This card is special, and it was given to me on my birthday. The card says, "Happy Birthday, Daddy," and it's signed by my two children.

Both five-dollar bills are worth the same amount, but they do not mean the same to me. The first bill was found; the second bill was given. This second bill, sent in the birthday card, means a whole lot to me because it was given to me by my children as an expression of love.

In fact, I'm not even sure I will spend this five dollars for anything; I may just keep it as a reminder of how nice and how loving my children acted toward me.

SS2824

Right now our planet Earth faces a terrible environmental problem. Perhaps you have learned about it on television, at school, or from your parents. The air is dirty and causes acid rain; a hole in the protective covering of the earth is letting in harmful rays from the sun; the temperatures are getting hotter; natural materials such as oil are running out; tropical rain forests are being cut down; many animals and plants are dying out; lakes, rivers, and streams are becoming polluted; garbage dumps are filling up; and the world is becoming overpopulated.

I think one reason we are having such big problems with the environment is that we are treating the earth as though we just found it (as I found the first five-dollar bill). Since we found it, we think the earth is ours, and we can do with it as we wish.

If we treated the earth as if it had been given to us rather than just had been found, we would not be mistreating it as we are. If we saw the earth as a creation of God (Genesis 1-2), we would treat it special and respect it. If we understood that God gave the earth as a gift and as an expression of love, we would take good care of it and would feel responsible to God for how we use it.

Whether we regard the earth as "found" or as "given" makes all the difference in the world!

Prayer:

> Loving and creative God, thank you for making the earth and all that is in it. We know you care about what you have made because you work for good and because you sent Jesus to save the world. The earth is yours, and everything that is in it. Help us to treat your earth as a gift given by you in love to us. Help us to regard it with respect. Forgive us if we have made the problem worse by what we have done to pollute the earth or by what we have let others do by our silence. These things we pray in the name of Jesus. Amen.

Pictures Can Be Revealing

Prop: A camera, preferably one with a flash, with no film in it

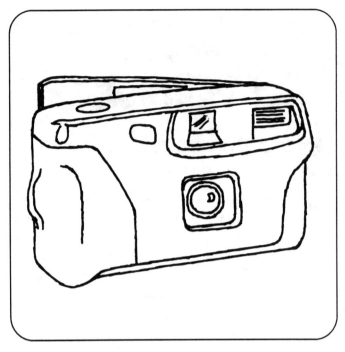

Do you recognize what I have in my hand? (Invite a response from the children.) It is a camera. Does your family have a camera? Have you ever used a camera? (Encourage responses to these questions.)

Cameras are very interesting. They take pictures of us where we are and indicate what we are doing. Perhaps we were standing beside a brother or a sister. Perhaps we were close by a pet, such as a dog or cat. Maybe we were at Grandma and Grandpa's for dinner or for a visit. Maybe we were playing with a friend.

Of course, we might not want a camera to take pictures of us all the time. There are times when we misbehave. Sometimes we do the things we shouldn't do, or we don't do the things we should do. We would not want to have pictures of those times!

God sees us all the time, whether we are being nice or whether we are being naughty. He sees us when we are at our best, and He sees us at our worst. God knows when we do right and when we do wrong. It's almost as if He has a camera which is always taking pictures of us, no matter what we are doing.

We should be thankful God is a loving God! He sees us just as we are, yet when we are truly sorry for what we have done or not done, God forgives us. He says to us, "I will remember your sins no longer." (See Isaiah 43:25.) Because God loves us, He forgives us.

Boys and girls, let's thank God for His love and forgiveness by trying to be the best we can be.

Prayer:

Kind and caring God, we give you thanks for loving us. You see us just as we are, and you know us better than we know ourselves (Psalm 139). You are always willing to forgive us when we do what we shouldn't, and when we don't do things we should. We are truly thankful for your forgiveness. Help us to do better. These things we pray in Jesus' name. Amen.

SS2824

The Risk of Striking Out

Props: A bat and a ball

I have two things with me which you may recognize and with which you may have played. What are these? (Show the bat and ball to the children and encourage them to answer.) How many of you have ever gone to a baseball game? (Encourage a show of hands.) Have you ever played baseball yourself? (Encourage the children to respond.)

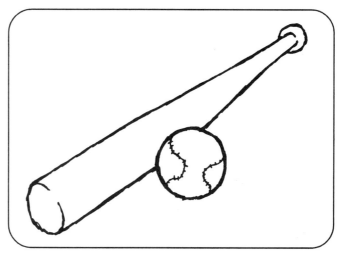

Have you ever seen a home run? (Encourage the children to answer.) Who has ever hit a home run yourself? (Ask for a show of hands.)

A home run is a very exciting moment in baseball. The ballplayer who hits one is very happy and excited, and the people who are watching are cheering and clapping.

What a thrill a home run is, but sometimes a baseball player strikes out! Even though he wants to hit a home run, he may miss three times in a row and fail. That is disappointing, not thrilling.

A person has to be willing to risk striking out in order to hit a home run. He has to take a chance of failing in order to be successful. Sometimes a home run will be hit; other times the person will not hit the ball at all. If a ballplayer wanted to take no chance at all of striking out, he would never put on a uniform and pick up a bat.

Even if you and I have never played baseball, never hit a home run, or never struck out, we still know success and failure. When we start learning how to count, we risk making mistakes. When we practice our spelling, we take a chance that we will fail to get all of the words right the first time or even the final time. When we try to read, we may find some words we don't know. When we try to color or to draw a picture, we might not do the kind of job we had hoped to do. When we sing, we may not hit all the right notes.

Unless we try, we will never be able to get something done right. Unless we take a chance of failing, we will never have success. Unless we risk striking out, we will never be able to hit a home run.

Prayer:

O, God, who encourages us to do the best we can, thank you for giving us minds to think and skills to develop. Help us to take the risks necessary for us to become everything you want us to be. In Jesus' name we pray. Amen.

God's Thermometer

Prop: An outside thermometer

I have with me an outside thermometer, girls and boys. (Display the thermometer to the children.) What does an outside thermometer do? (Let children answer.) The thermometer measures the temperature of the air. By looking at an outside thermometer, we can tell how hot or cold it is.

If the thermometer reads 20°, is the weather hot or cold? (Let children respond.) When it's only 20°, the weather is cold. If the outside thermometer reads 98°, is the weather hot or cold? (Let children answer.) When it is 98°, the weather is hot.

A thermometer tells us the temperature. We can know how hot or how cold it is by looking at an outside thermometer's numbers. By paying close attention to the thermometer, we know what the weather is like.

In a similar way, the Bible acts as a thermometer to tell us what God is like. The Bible records the ways God has dealt with human beings in history. The Bible tells us that God made the world and saw that it was good, and that God made people and saw that they were good. The Bible tells us that God so loved the world and us that He sent Jesus. The Bible tells us that God wants us to be kind because God is kind. The Bible tells us that God always acts fairly, lovingly, and forgivingly.

By looking at an outside thermometer, we know what the weather is like. By looking at the Bible, we know what God is like.

Prayer:

> Great God of all the ages, we praise you, and we thank you for being the kind of God you are. You are willing to forgive us, rather than to seek revenge; you value us, instead of regarding us as worthless; and you love us so much that you gave us your Son. We marvel and are amazed at the kind of God you are, and we ask you to help us be more like you. We ask it in the name of Him who loved all people, Jesus Christ our Lord and Savior. Amen.

Sending the Message

Prop: A small piece of notepad paper on which a message has been written

What is this? (Hold up the paper and encourage the children to answer.) It is a small piece of paper. In fact, it is a small piece of notepad paper, and there is a message on it. Let's see what it says: "Don't forget to call your sister and check to make sure she knows what time you will be arriving at her house." That's the message, and I'll be sure to call my sister!

Let's pretend that I wanted to give someone a message. If I wanted to let someone know something, how might I do that? How do you think I could send the message? (Encourage the children to think of ways to send messages.)

Those are good answers, boys and girls. (Pick up on some of their answers in continuing the story.) I could write the message on a piece of paper, and send it to the person who could read my message.

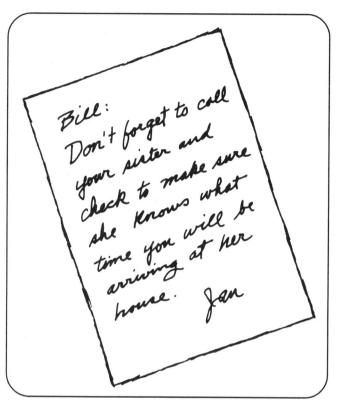

Bill:
Don't forget to call your sister and check to make sure she knows what time you will be arriving at her house.
Jan

I could send someone to deliver my message. That person could tell my message to the other person for me. That way, the individual for whom the message was meant could receive it "personally"!

I could go. I could give the person the message myself.

SS2824

Girls and boys, we have at least three ways of sending my message.

Did you know that God has used those very same three ways to send us the message that He loves us?

In the Bible, God gives us a written message. On those pages, we can read (or have someone read to us) what He wants to tell us.

God also sent people to carry His message to us. These people were called "prophets." They spoke in God's behalf; in fact, it was God's very own Word they told.

Most importantly, God came in the person of Jesus Christ to give us His message personally. Through Jesus we receive the clearest and most joyous message of all–God loves us.

He has told us in all three ways that He loves you, me, and everyone. Now isn't that a happy message? I'm glad God sent it.

Prayer:

Great God of all times, all places, and all people, we thank you for constantly trying to communicate with us. We know that you are always seeking to have your message "of good tidings and great joy" received by your human creations. Thank you for giving us the Bible, for sending the prophets, and for coming yourself in Jesus. May we hear loud and clear your message of love! We ask it in Jesus' name. Amen.

White Lines

Prop: A picture or a drawing of a highway with white or yellow lines on the sides of the road

Girls and boys, I want you to look careful-ly at this picture. What do you see along the sides of the road? (Encourage the chil-dren to respond.) There are white lines along the sides of the road. Why do you think those lines are there? (Encourage the children to use their imaginations.) The lines follow the road and tell you when the car is near the edge. You can see the lines at night when the car lights shine on them.

You shared very good answers! The lines are on the road to let drivers know where the edge of the road is. This is very im-portant especially at night or in a fog. The lines help drivers drive safely, stay on the road, and know which way to go.

Sometimes we may feel as if we are living our lives in a fog. We are not sure what we ought to do; we are confused. When people treat us badly, we may think about getting back at them rather than "not repay evil with evil." (See Romans 12:17.) Some people do not tell the truth and get away with it; should we do the same? Other people cheat and steal and appear to get ahead. Is being fair and being honest really better?

Fortunately, we Christians have help in clearing up the confusion. We have someone to show us the way. We have His words to guide us and to keep us on the proper path.

That someone, of course, is Jesus. Jesus' life and words point the way. He showed us that we should forgive our enemies. He told people the truth would set them free. (See John 8:32.) His fairness and kindness in dealing with others act like "white lines on the high-way" to keep us "on the road"" and to let us know "which way to go."

The white lines on the edge of a highway help a driver drive safely. Jesus' example and teachings help a Christian stay safely on God's "road."

Prayer:

God of the covenant, thank you for your guidance in life, especially during those times when things seem very confusing. Thank you for the gift of Jesus, who clears things up for us by teaching us how to live. Thank you for your Spirit, who prompts us to focus on Jesus and to stay on the right road. In Jesus' name. Amen.

Going Fishing

Props: A fishing rod and reel, complete with fishing line and lure

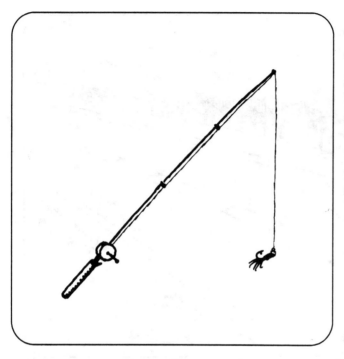

What do I have with me? (Show the children the rod and reel, and encourage answers from them.) It is a fishing pole. How many of you have ever gone fishing? (Ask for a show of hands.) Did you catch any fish? (Encourage responses from the children.)

This fishing rod and reel have several parts, each of which is very important. The rod or pole is important because it gives the person who is fishing something to hold on to as he pulls a hooked fish out of the water. If the fish is large, the rod will bend when the fish is brought from the water. (Demonstrate.)

The fishing line is also very important. It attaches to the reel and allows the one who is fishing to attract fish close at hand or a long way off. The line must be strong, so the weight of a fish does not break the line. (Point to the line and indicate its connections to the reel and to the lure).

The reel is also very important, because it allows the fisherman to bring the hooked fish nearer before pulling it out of the water. By turning the crank, the fisherman brings the fish closer to the riverbank or the seashore. (Demonstrate.)

The lure and hook are also very important. The lure draws the fish to the hook, and then the hook catches the fish. Without the lure, the fish would not pay any attention to the hook, and without the hook, the lure would not be able to catch the fish. (Help the children understand by showing the lure and hook to them.)

The rod or pole, the fishing line, the reel, and the lure and hook are all very important. All parts are needed in order to catch fish.

Jesus told His followers to go into the world and make disciples of all people (Matthew 28:19). He told them he would make them "fishers of men" (Mark 1:17). Helping people to become Christians is like fishing.

In our "fishing" for new Christians, the Bible is like our fishing rod or pole. The Bible gives us something to hold on to.

The fishing line is like God. God brings people to us so we can share His love with them and "bring them in" to His family.

The reel is like the Holy Spirit. He brings a person closer "to the shore." The Holy Spirit speaks to people and helps them receive Jesus as Savior.

The lure and its hook are like Jesus. Jesus' love attracts people to God, and commitment, getting "hooked," is their response to what He has done for them.

The fishing rod or pole (the Bible), the fishing line (God), the reel (the Holy Spirit), and the lure and hook (Jesus) are all very important. All four are needed for us to be "fishers of men."

Prayer:

> God, whose love knows no exceptions and whose grace knows no boundaries, thank you for the privilege we have of sharing the Good News of Jesus Christ. We also thank you for helping us in our efforts to be "fishermen." Help us to be both active and patient as we "fish" for people. We ask all these things in Jesus' name. Amen.

SS2824

Like a Windup Toy

Prop: A mechanical toy which runs on a windup spring. (The talk may be adapted to focus on a toy which uses a battery for power.)

I have one of my favorite toys with me. Do you know what this is? (Show the children the toy and encourage their answers.) This is a toy cat. I call her "Jungle Cat." Let me show you how Jungle Cat works: you wind her up; put her on the floor; push the "on" button; and she walks, pounces, growls, and turns her head from side to side. (Demonstrate the diverse actions of the windup toy.)

Jungle Cat is a windup toy. I wind her up, and I let her go. She does the rest on her own. I simply watch from a distance.

Some people think the world is like a windup toy. They believe that in the beginning God wound it up and then let it go. They think the world does the rest from a distance.

This belief sees God as the Creator of the world, but it does not see God close to us and active in the world. The Bible teaches us that God cares and that He is ". . . an ever-present help in trouble" (Psalm 46:1). The Bible teaches us that God works for good and for peace in the world, freeing those who are held down and lifting up those who are put down.

God was so concerned about the world, that He came down to be one of us! Through Jesus He became involved in the lives of people.

God's relationship to the world and us is not the same as my relationship to Jungle Cat. God does not treat the world like a windup toy. He cares; and that means He is loving, is close at hand, and is involved.

Prayer:

Almighty and caring God, your power and your majesty are tremendous! Your power is revealed in the creation and in the Resurrection of Jesus of Nazareth. Your majesty is shown in the beauty of nature and in the beauty of human beings. You are not a Creator who remains afar. You are not one who sees only from a distance. You are with us caring and guiding. Thank you for your love. Thank you for responding to our prayers, petitions, and plights. In the name of Jesus. Amen.

More Secure than a Silo

Prop: A silo (a model from a child's play set, a picture from a magazine, or a drawing)

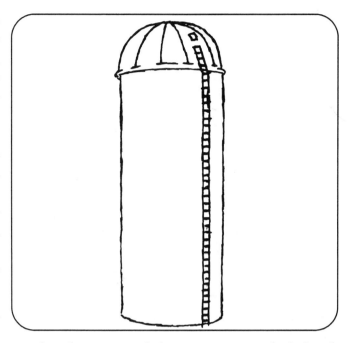

Boys and girls, I have something with me which you may recognize if you ever lived on a farm or if you have been out in the car with your family driving in the country. What is this? (Encourage answers.) It is a silo. How is a silo used? (Encourage responses from the children.) A silo is used to store what a farmer has grown in his fields. Usually silos are filled with hay, corn, or other grain.

A farmer's silo contains what is very valuable to the farmer. The crops he has grown are stored there. A farmer's success and money depend on what's in the silo.

Your mothers' and fathers' success and money depend not on what is in silos but on what is in their bank accounts. The money they have stored there represents their hard work.

Neither the grain stored in the silo nor the money kept in the bank is perfectly safe. Mice and other small animals and crop diseases can destroy the crops kept in the silos. Bank robbers and something called "inflation" (which means that the money loses some of its value–it's worth less as a result) can make the money in the bank disappear.

Jesus tells us that what's really valuable and makes us successful is our "treasures in heaven." (See Matthew 6:19-21.) "Treasures in heaven" means deeds of kindness and charity done on earth. By being nice, loving, and helpful, a person is storing up "treasures in heaven"!

Being nice and doing good things–our "treasures in heaven"–are more important than what is in a silo or a bank account. They are also more secure, for no one or nothing can take them away. Let's store up treasures in heaven, where moth and rust won't destroy, and where thieves can't break in and steal. If our treasure is in heaven, that's where our hearts will be. (See Matthew 6:20-21.)

Prayer:

> Gracious God, you have shown us what is good and lasting: we are to love you and to love our neighbors as ourselves. In so doing, we are obedient to your will and pleasing in your sight. Help us store up "treasures in heaven" by doing kind and caring deeds in your name. Help us place our treasures and our hearts where there is true and eternal security–with you! In Jesus' name. Amen.

High-Wire Act

Props: A stuffed animal (for example, a teddy bear), a length of rope, and an adhesive bandage

I have brought a "friend" with me, a teddy bear named "Molly." Molly is a very special animal, for she walks the high wire. Let me show you what I mean. (Request two volunteers to hold the ends of the rope, which is to be stretched taut at a position where everyone can see.)

Molly will now walk the high wire. (Hold the stuffed animal and make it "walk" along the top of the rope.) Molly is actually pretty good at this! (Let the stuffed animal fall off the rope onto the floor.) Oh, no! Molly has taken a tumble!

(Pick up the stuffed animal, "comforting" it.) There, there, Molly, it's all right. (To the children) I think that she has hurt her knee. It looks as if she has scraped it. (Recruit a volunteer to hold the stuffed animal, while you place the adhesive bandage on its knee.) I think Molly will be okay now.

Sometimes you, too, get hurt: you fall down and skin a knee; you feel bad because things did not go your way; someone is not nice to you and hurts your feelings; you fail at something important to you and are disappointed.

Fortunately, your parents pick you up, put bandages on you, comfort you, and tell you that everything is going to be okay. That makes you feel better.

Also fortunately, God helps to pick us up, makes us feel better, comforts us, and gives us hope that everything is going to be okay. God is like a loving parent who cares for us.

God and our parents love us and care about us when we are hurt and all the rest of the time, too.

Prayer:

Gracious God, who loves us and cares about us, we thank you that at every moment of our lives you are prepared to pick us up and help us feel better. We are thankful also for our parents, relatives, and friends who care about us. Help us to be willing to give of ourselves to those who need us. These things we pray in the name of Jesus Christ, who always stopped to help those in need. Amen.

SS2824

Checking the Plates

Prop: A license plate

I have with me something which is on your family's car and on all cars on the streets and roads. Do you recognize what this is? (Hold up the license plate for all to see.) It is a license plate! Do you remember what color the license plate on your family's car is? (Encourage the children to respond.) The license plate I have here is _____. Now for a really hard question: do you remember the number on your license plate? (Encourage the children to respond.) The number on this license plate is _____. It is for the state of _____. What is the name of the state on your license plate? (Encourage the children to volunteer answers.)

A license plate, by the color, the number, and the name of the state, can help us learn who the owner of the car is. No one else has a license plate exactly like this one. Who a person is–his name and address–can be discovered by the information on a license plate.

Christians also give out information about themselves. They are known not by color or number or state, but by the way they act. Christians are filled with joy (because they know God loves them), are kinder than necessary (because that's the way Jesus wants them to be), and are forgiving of people (because God in Christ forgave them). When others see us acting in these ways, they know that we are Christians.

If someone were watching you, would that person recognize you as Christians? We all have faults and shortcomings, but hopefully, most times they would say, "See how kindly those persons are acting! We know they are Christians by their love."

Prayer:

> Gracious and loving God, we know who you are by your Word and your great acts in the world– your creation of the world (and us), your forgiveness through Jesus, and your caring about us. Help us to be known as Christians by our joy, kindness, and forgiveness. As Christ showed love to us, may we show love to others. We ask it in His name. Amen.

Flying

Prop: A model airplane

I have with me a model of something that I think you will recognize. What is this? (Show the model airplane to the children and encourage them to respond.) It is an airplane. (If you are familiar with some of the details of the particular airplane model you are using in your story, and if time permits, share some of this information with the children.)

Perhaps the most basic and amazing thing about an airplane is that it can fly. It is marvelous to watch a plane move down a runway, gather speed, and then rise into the air.

How does an airplane fly? What does it take to get the plane into the air? (Guide the children in their responses to these questions.) Those are good answers! Let's think about some of them.

An airplane can fly because it has a motor, wings, fuel, pilot, and a propellor. The motor gives the plane power, the wings allow the plane to ride along on the air, the fuel keeps the motor going, the pilot steers the plane, and the propellor pulls the plane ahead.

All of these are needed if the airplane is going to fly. A plane without a motor will go nowhere; without wings, the plane cannot rise into the air; without fuel, the motor cannot run; without a pilot, the plane would go the wrong way and probably crash; without a propellor to pull the plane ahead, the plane would just sit on the ground.

The church is somewhat like an airplane: it needs the same things a plane does in order to "fly." Like a plane, the church needs a motor: faith is the motor of the church. It is what gives it power. A church without faith will go nowhere.

Love is the wings of the church. Love gives the church the ability to rise up and be what God wants it to be. A church without love will sink down and be nothing like what it should be.

Service is the fuel that keeps the motor of the church running. Sometimes called "missions," service fuels the faith of the church.

Jesus Christ is the pilot of the church. His actions and His instructions guide the church in the proper direction. With Jesus at the controls, the church will stay on course.

God (working through the Holy Spirit) is the propellor of the church. God pulls the church ahead–helping it, purifying it, and inspiring it. A church without God goes nowhere.

An airplane needs a motor, wings, fuel, a pilot, and a propellor. Without all of these, the plane will be unable to fly. In order for the church to "fly," it needs faith, love, service, Jesus, and God. Without all of these, the church, too, will be grounded!

Prayer:

> God, it is amazing and marvelous that a plane can fly. It is also amazing and mar-velous that the church can "fly" and be what you want it to be. We confess that some-times we have not helped the church get off the ground–we have not loved others as we should, and we have been unwilling to think of serving others. At times our faith has wavered, and we have not paid enough attention to where Jesus is steering us and the direction in which you are pulling us. Help the church to "fly" as you want us to. In Jesus' name we pray. Amen.

It's What's on the Inside That Counts

Props: Two packages—one brightly and colorfully wrapped, but with "undesirable objects" inside; the other unattractively wrapped, but containing lollipops

Today I am going to give you a choice, boys and girls. Would you like to have what is inside this beautifully wrapped package or what is inside this plainly wrapped package? (Solicit responses by a show of hands.)

Let's see what's inside this colorfully wrapped package. (Take out objects, such as a dirty sock, a banana peel, a wad of already-chewed bubble gum, an empty yogurt container, and a candy bar wrapper with no candy bar.) You look surprised!

Now let's see what's in this unattractively wrapped package. (Take out a big bag of lollipops.) Are you surprised?

Things are not always what they seem to be, and neither are people. Sometimes a person who is good-looking on the outside is not very nice on the inside. Sometimes a person who owns a lot of things and dresses in the best of clothes is not a nice person. Sometimes a person may be unwilling to share with others.

Girls and boys, it's what's on the inside that counts! God wants us to value people for their love, honesty, and good attitudes. That's what really matters, not what they look like.

I'm going to give each of you a lollipop. As you enjoy it, let it remind you that it's what's on the inside that counts.

Prayer:

> God, who loves us, you have given each of us the gift of life. We thank you for this gift, and we pray that you would help us see others as they really are. Remind us that the love, honesty, and friendliness of a person are what really matter. In Jesus' name we pray. Amen.

Warning Signs

Prop: Pictures of signs which warn of hazards on the road

I have some signs with me that I would like you to help me read. What do they say? (Encourage children to answer.) "Watch Ice on Bridge," "Slippery When Wet," "Soft Shoulder," "Drive Slow– Work Crew Ahead."

These signs tell us when there are things about which we need to be concerned. The bridge could be slick in cold weather; the road will probably be slippery if it's been raining; there is soft ground on the side of the road; and there are people working ahead. Without these signs, we could have an accident or take unwise chances. These signs are called "warning signs," for they warn us of something ahead of which we need to be aware.

In a similar way, the Holy Spirit gives us warning signs which tell us of danger ahead. When we are not living as we should, these signs warn us of something of which we need to be aware. The Holy Spirit "pricks" our consciences to make us feel guilty when we do wrong. He makes us feel uncomfortable when we are tempted to disobey our parents.

As the warning signs on the road tell us to look out and to take care, these warning signs from the Holy Spirit tell us to be careful with our lives and to change some of the things we're doing so that we can be happy and pleasing to God.

Prayer:

> God, our Father and Friend, thank you for caring enough about us to send us warning signs when we are moving dangerously toward high risk or harm. Make us mindful of the Holy Spirit's warning signs and wise enough to change our ways if we are headed for trouble. These things we pray in Jesus' name. Amen.

Help Us to Remember

Prop: A picture of a pet no longer living

I want to share this picture with you. (Display the picture so that all may see.) This a picture of a dog. Her name is "Bianca," and she is no longer living. She died not too long ago at the age of fifteen. (The storyteller should show a picture and tell about a pet of his or her own.)

Looking at this picture and thinking about Bianca makes me remember when she was just a little puppy. She was so small that I could hold her in one hand. When we left with her from the kennel, she whimpered because she was leaving behind her mother and her brothers and sisters. I remember how closely she snuggled to me while riding in the car.

As she grew, she began to enjoy cuddling beside me whenever she had a chance. She delighted in returning sticks I would throw for her. She never needed to be on a leash, for she would follow right beside me wherever I went.

What joy Bianca added to my life! I recall this whenever I see her picture. Pictures help us to remember.

When we Christians see the bread and the cup for Communion, we think of Jesus. They help us to remember Him–who He is and what He did. The bread and the cup help us to remember that He was God's Son helping, teaching, healing, and loving. We are reminded that He suffered on a cross for you and me, and that His story did not end in a tomb. All of these memories come to us when we see the bread and the cup and think of Jesus.

A picture of a dog and a picture of a Communion table with the bread and the cup on it are both things that help us to remember.

Prayer:

God, of the past, the present, and the future, we rejoice that you have given so much to us. Though we don't deserve it, you have bestowed good gifts upon us–even the greatest gift of all, Jesus. Thank you for caring so much that you sent Jesus Christ into the world to be born, to teach and heal, to die for our sins, and to be raised from the dead. Thank you also that we have minds which can remember what Jesus did for us. We are grateful that things we see can help us remember what's so very important. These things we pray in Jesus' name. Amen.

What Makes Life Worth Living?

Prop: A flower or a plant

Boys and girls, I brought something with me this morning which I'm sure you recognize. What is it? (Children: "A flower." "A plant.") You're right! I have a beautiful flower/plant to show you.

What does this flower/plant need to stay alive and to grow? (Encourage responses, such as "sunshine, water, food from the soil, and care.") A flower/ plant needs sunshine and water and food from the soil and good care. *Good care* means that we make sure it gets enough sun and water and all the other things it needs.

Let me ask you another question: What do you and I need to stay alive and grow? (Solicit responses, such as "a home, clothing, food, love.") You and I need a place to live, clothes to wear, food to eat, and love to support us. Because your parents love you, they try to give you a nice home, buy you nice clothes, and put good food on the table.

Like growing plants, people need love and care. It's love that makes life worth living!

Prayer:

    O, God, who is the source of care and love, we give you thanks for all that our parents do for us. Most of all, we are thankful that they do all those things for us because they love us. Help us live and grow in such a way that we please you and show our gratitude to our fathers and mothers. In the name of Jesus, who grew in wisdom and stature and in favor with you and others, we pray. Amen.

Sticking Together

Props: Some pieces of paper which collectively have a picture of a house or of some other easily recognizable subject, some hidden glue, a sheet of paper for background, and a small desk on which to work

Today I have some pieces of paper with me. If we put them together, I think we'll be able to see what picture all of the pieces make. What can we use to help the pieces of paper stay together? (Encourage answers from the children.) We could use paste or glue.

(Get the hidden glue and, with the help of the children, fit the pieces together on the small desk in order to reveal the complete picture.) What do you see? (Encourage responses from the children.) That's right! It is a house!

(Glue the pieces together on the sheet of paper.) Glue is very useful. It makes things stay together.

Boys and girls, there's something else like glue, something that helps people stay together. You can't see it; it's invisible; you can see only what it does.

Girls and boys, it's love. Love is what holds families together, joins friends together, and keeps mothers and fathers together. Girls and boys, love helps us stick together.

Prayer:

> Eternal God, we give you thanks for love–the love that families share, the love between friends, the love which fathers and mothers have for each other, and the love which you have for us. Help us to stick together, God. We ask it in Jesus' name. Amen.

SS2824

What You Cannot See

Prop: A portable radio, pre-tuned to a music station and placed out of sight, but easily accessible

Girls and boys, there are some things around us which we cannot see. Right now, for example, there are waves of music floating through the air. We cannot see them, but they are there.

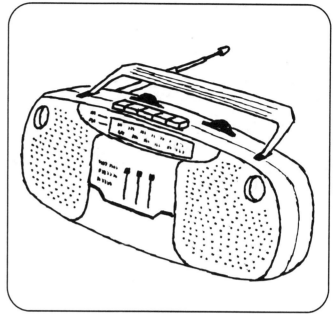

Let me show you what I mean. (Show the radio to the children.) What do I have here? This is a radio. Let's turn it on. (Do so.) What do you hear? (Encourage responses from the children.) We are hearing music. This music comes from waves which are broadcast, or sent through the air. These waves are tuned in, "caught" we might say, by the radio receiver. As a result, we hear music. We cannot see those music waves, but that doesn't mean that they aren't there. In fact, we believe that the waves are there because of what happens on the radio.

Boys and girls, we cannot see God, but that doesn't mean He isn't there. In fact, we believe that God is there because of what happens to us and to the world. We see love bringing people together; we ourselves feel loved and accepted; we see people who are angry at each other apologize and become friends again; we see a person who has been wronged by another find the power from somewhere to forgive that person, and we see people who have experienced some very difficult times discover the strength to keep going and to keep hoping.

We cannot see God, but we can see Him working in people's lives.

Prayer:

Kind and loving God, we give you thanks that you are here with us, even though we cannot see you with our eyes. We do see what you do, and we see how people and the world are affected. Thank you for caring about us and loving us. In Jesus' name we pray. Amen.

Trust

Props: The children themselves and some adult members of the congregation

Today I am going to ask you to do something for me: I would like each one of you to walk into the congregation and choose someone whom you do not know to come back with you to the front. (Walk with the children and encourage them to select an adult to walk with them to their original starting point.)

Girls and boys, how did it feel to do what I asked you to do? (Encourage responses from the children based on their experiences: "I felt scared," "I didn't want to do it," "I didn't know whom to choose.") I understand that it wasn't an easy thing for you to do. You don't know all of the people who were sitting there. You had to trust a person you did not know.

Why did you choose the person you did? (Encourage responses from the children regarding their criteria of selection: "I had seen this person before," "He seemed very nice," "My mommy is friends with her.") I see what you're saying to me: the people you chose were not complete strangers to you, or those people made you feel at ease because they smiled at you or appeared to be kind.

Trusting someone is not an easy thing to do! It is a bit scary, and it may make us feel very uncomfortable. It is easier to trust when we know something—even just a little bit—about a person. A face that you've seen before or a warm smile on a face that's new to you can be enough to make you feel more comfortable and more trusting.

Boys and girls, God asks us to trust Him. That may not be easy. We've never seen God; we've never seen His face. How do we know God is trustworthy?

We know God is trustworthy because in Jesus we have seen what God is really like: He is a God of love, who cares about each one of us. He is a God of faithfulness, upon whom we can depend. He is a God of forgiveness, who doesn't keep a record of how bad we've been, but wipes the slate clean and gives us a second chance. When we think of Jesus, we know that we believe in a God who can be trusted. When we think about the caring, loving, forgiving Jesus, we know that we can trust His heavenly Father, our God.

Prayer:

> God, who sent us Jesus, thank you that through your Son's life we learn about the kind of God you are—a God who cares, a God who is reliable, a God who doesn't seek revenge. Help us trust in you. This we pray in the name of Jesus Christ, our Lord. Amen.

Holding It All Together

Prop: An unassembled plastic model (for example: car, boat, plane)

How many of you like to put together plastic models of cars, boats, or planes? (Encourage a show of hands by the children.) What is your favorite thing to put together? (Encourage answers from the children.)

I have with me a model of a car. (Show the children.) It is not yet put together and is in this box. Let's take a look inside. (Do so.) Look at all the pieces! How many pieces do you think are in here? (Encourage answers.)

All of these pieces fit together to form the model car. What will stick them together and keep them that way? (Encourage the children to respond.) A special kind of glue will hold the pieces together. Without the glue, the pieces would remain as individual parts, separate from each other. With the glue, the pieces will stay together, and a neat model will result. The glue is really important!

God is really important to Christians, boys and girls! He is the glue that holds things together. When sin separated people from God, God sent Jesus to bring us back together again. When people are separated from each other by anger or hurt, God works to bring them together in love and forgiveness.

Glue will hold all the pieces of the model together. God is the glue that holds people together with Him and with each other.

Prayer:

Eternal and loving God, thank you for caring enough to send Jesus, so that we would not have to be separated from you by our sins. Thank you also for working to bring people together. These things we pray in Jesus' name. Amen.

Button, Button

Prop: A shirt or jacket which has buttons to keep the front closed

Girls and boys, what is this? (Solicit answers from the children.) You're right; it's a shirt (jacket).

I think I'll try it on. Hmm, let's see, first this arm, then this arm. Now it's comfortable, but how will I close up the front? How will the two sides be held together? (Encourage the children to respond.) The buttons on the front will join the two sections and keep them together.

Buttons are very important! Without buttons, I would have problems keeping this shirt (jacket) on. Without all these buttons keeping the front closed, the wind would get in, and I would get cold. Each button must be sewn on securely. If a button gets too loose or falls off, it cannot do its job. A button must be firmly anchored. Buttons are very small, but they do a big job.

You know, boys and girls, sometimes people do not get along well with each other; sometimes they get upset with each other. Occasionally people are separated by anger, misunderstanding, jealousy, or hurt. Sometimes people who feel this way will not come around each other, or even talk to each other. They are like the front of a shirt (jacket) which cannot be joined.

What is needed is someone to act as a button to pull the two together. We call this drawing together "reconciliation," which means the act of becoming friends again. For a person to act as a button, to be a "reconciler," he must be firmly anchored in Jesus. A person must be secure in Jesus Christ in order to have the courage, patience, and persistence to be successful in bringing two people together.

Buttons are very important. People who act as buttons, as reconcilers, are very important, too. We need to ask Jesus to guide us and help us as we try to bring people back together in His name.

Prayer:

Gracious God, through Jesus Christ you reconciled the world to yourself. We know that you can help in situations where people have separated themselves from each other. Help us to be your agents of reconciliation, bringing people together again in love and forgiveness. In Jesus' name. Amen.

Too Much

Prop: A suitcase or other travel bag stuffed to overflowing

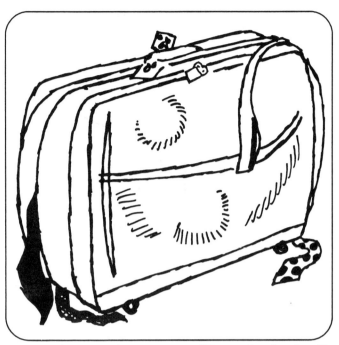

How many of you like to travel? (Encourage a show of hands.) How many of you enjoy going with your families on vacation? (Again, encourage a response.)

Well, then, I'm sure that you've seen one of these. (Display the suitcase.) What is the matter with it? (Encourage children to respond. For example, "It has clothes sticking out," "There's too much in it.") Let's take a look inside.

There's a lot in here! There are socks, shoes, shirts, and pants. I think I've tried to pack in too many things.

A suitcase holds only so much. Taking more than I really need doesn't make sense. The suitcase is bulging. If I try to get more clothes in, either the clothes will fall out or the suitcase will be damaged. I need to know when to say "Enough, that's all; I'll take no more."

Jesus told a story about a man who felt he never had enough (Luke 12:16-21). He built bigger and bigger barns to hold everything he thought he needed, but even that did not seem to satisfy him. Jesus called this man foolish and warned that it is not wise for anyone to gain the whole world, but in the "getting" to lose his own soul (Mark 8:36).

We, too, can be foolish when we accumulate too much or eat too much or drink too much. We can be like suitcases that are filled to bursting. We need to remember to take only what we need and to know when to say "Enough." We must be wise and find our happiness not in what we have, but in what we do for others.

Prayer:

> Heavenly Father, the giver of all good and precious gifts, thank you that you care about us. We are sorry that we sometimes confuse what we need with what we want. Help us to say "Enough" and to live lives of giving, not getting. We want to be wise, not foolish. These things we pray in Jesus' name. Amen.

Money Can't Buy Love

Prop: A $20 bill, wadded-up so that it fits in the palm of a closed hand

I have something in my hand which can get me several things I want. What do I have here? (Encourage responses). I have a $20 bill.

What do you suppose I could buy with this $20 bill? (Encourage ideas from the children). I could buy a shirt. I could buy tickets to a ball game. I could buy some books or a couple of games. I could buy a doll or a stuffed animal. I could buy a *lot* of things with this money.

Of course, money cannot buy me everything! Money cannot buy true friends. Money cannot buy complete happiness. Money cannot buy self-confidence. Money cannot buy me love. Money cannot buy YOU love!

Your moms and dads love you just because you're you. Even if you could buy their love with money, you wouldn't need to. You are already loved.

Money cannot buy God's love either. God loved us so much that He sent Jesus to die for us. Jesus showed us how to love one another. Girls and boys, you can't buy God's love; it's freely given.

Money can buy some things, but money can't buy everything: money can't buy love!

Prayer:

God of never-ending, ever-present love, thank you for loving us with no conditions attached. Because you love us as we are, we know that we are worthwhile and important to you. Help us to share your love with other people. In the name of Jesus Christ we pray. Amen.

SS2824

Flying Together

Prop: A picture or drawing of geese flying in a "V" formation

I brought a picture with me, and I wonder if you can guess what it is. (Encourage responses.) It is a picture of birds, but what kind of birds are these? They are geese.

How many of you have been outdoors and have seen and heard geese flying overhead? (Encourage a show of hands.) Depending on how low they are flying, they can be quite noisy, with their loud "honking"!

The geese in the picture I have with me are flying in a certain way, a certain formation. What letter of the alphabet does their way of flying, their formation, look like? (Encourage answers from the children.) It is a *V*. Geese fly in a formation which is the shape of a *V*.

Geese fly this way for a special reason: stronger geese fly at the front of the *V*, and weaker geese fly at the back. (Point this out.) The stronger, faster geese fly at the front because their strength and speed part the air and make it easier for the weaker geese who fly behind. The weaker, slower geese are helped by the stronger, faster geese.

Why do you think geese do all that honking? The geese honk to encourage each other. The slower geese are encouraged by the honking of the geese in front of them. If one of the geese is tired or in trouble, this encouragement is very important to help it keep up with the flock.

I think this story about geese is very important for us humans to remember! If geese help each other, humans should help each other, too. People who "have" should help those who "have not"; people who are stronger ought to help those who are weaker.

This may mean sharing a toy with someone who doesn't have one, standing up for someone who is being bullied by an unkind person, or helping someone do something or understand something that is difficult for him.

Geese fly together, encouraging and helping each other. Can we human beings do any less?

Prayer:

God, who created us and who wants to bring out the best in us, we give you thanks for the living things you have made. We especially marvel at the flying geese and are moved by the way they help each other. Help us to do the same. We ask this in Jesus' name, remembering that He went about helping others and wants us to do the same. Amen.

SS2824

Masks

Prop: A mask (not too scary!)

I have something which I know you will recognize. (Hold up the mask.) What is this? (Encourage the children to respond.) This is a mask. Let me put it on so you can see how it looks. (Do so; if time permits, you could also put it on some of the children.)

How many of you like to dress up in costumes and put on masks? (Encourage a show of hands.) What do you like to dress up as? (If children need prompting, offer some suggestions: a pirate, a football player, a scarecrow, a cheerleader, an angel, a tiger, a cowboy.) It's fun to pretend. It's fun to make believe that we're pirates or scarecrows or tigers! It's fun to pretend that we are something that we are not.

You know, girls and boys, God loves each of us just as we are. We pretend for fun, but we *don't* have to pretend to be something else to make God like us. We don't have to try to be something that we're not, to gain God's love. No, God sees us just as we really are–and He loves us!

Prayer:

Kind and loving God, you see us just the way we are, and you love us. You know that we are not perfect; you know that too often we do unloving things. Yet, you love us! We thank you for seeing beyond our most noticeable faults and finding something of value in us. Help us to do the same with each other. This we pray in Jesus' name. Amen.

SS2824

A Chairy Tale

Prop: A four-legged chair

Girls and boys, at breakfast this morning you probably sat on one of these. (Display the chair.) A chair is a very useful thing to have. What do you use chairs for in your house? To sit-on during meals? To watch television? To sit at your desk or a table and draw?

How many of you have accidentally fallen off a chair? (Encourage a show of hands.) Perhaps you fell off because you were rocking back and forth on the chair. Maybe you were not positioned properly on the seat of the chair, and your weight caused the chair to tip to one side.

Look at the bottom of this chair, boys and girls. It has four legs. Each one of these legs is necessary for the chair to stand upright. If one of the legs is missing, or even wobbly, the chair will be very dangerous.

If three of the legs have been taken off, or are unstable, the chair won't be useful at all. A chair needs four legs in order to remain upright and do its job.

Our Christian lives are somewhat like chairs: they need four legs on which to stand. The first leg is *faith*. Our faith as Christians involves giving ourselves to God and trusting in Him. Faith is very important, but it is not the only leg that holds up our Christian lives.

The second leg is *hope*. God is trustworthy and caring, and we believe that God is never far from us. As a result, we live with the hope that God is working to make things better. No matter how bad things get, God will help them improve.

The third leg is *love*. Jesus said that all of God's commandments together mean we should love God and love other people. Loving others means trying to be kind to them and putting them first.

SS2824

The fourth leg is *charity*. We should share what we have with those who need it. Charity is sharing. We are willing to share because God loved all of us so much that He shared His Son with us.

Chairs are held up by four legs. Our Christian lives are held upright by four legs, too: *faith* (giving ourselves to God), *hope* (trusting God to do what's best), *love* (giving of ourselves to others), and *charity* (sharing what we have).

Prayer:

Faithful and loving God, you are willing to give of yourself. In fact, when we needed it most of all, you sent your Son so that the world would not be condemned, but saved. Help us to "stand" in faith, hope, love, and charity. In Jesus' name. Amen.

Shining Star Publications, Copyright © 1992, A Division of Good Apple

SS2824

Getting Rid of the Dirt

Props: A portable, electric vacuum cleaner and a small portion of dirt

I have a powerful machine here! Let me show you what I mean. (Put dirt on floor.) Now isn't that a mess? The carpet needs to be made clean again. I'll turn on this machine (do so) and run the nozzle through the dirt. There! The vacuum cleaner removed the dirt from the floor.

I suppose that each one of you has seen a vacuum cleaner before. Have you ever used one yourself? (Encourage responses from the children.) A vacuum cleaner has enough suction to take away the dirt from the carpet and make the floor clean again.

Boys and girls, sometimes our lives are like dirty floors. We do not always do what we are supposed to do; we do what we are not supposed to do. We are supposed to share, but we keep what we have for ourselves. We are supposed to forgive, but we hold a grudge and seek revenge. We are supposed to care about others, but too often we act as if we don't care. We make promises that we break. We become angry and forget to be patient. We think we will be happy if we own a lot of things.

Our lives need to be cleaned up! Fortunately, Jesus Christ takes away our sins. He accepts us just as we are, forgives us, gets rid of our dirt, and then helps us do better. Jesus is like a powerful vacuum cleaner which makes us clean again.

Prayer:

Eternal God, thank you for Jesus. He loves us, cares about us, and forgives us. We need Him to get rid of the dirt in our lives and make us clean again. We believe that Jesus' power is enough to change us and help us become the kind of people you want us to be. In Jesus' name. Amen.

SS2824

A Special Message

Props: A postcard, a letter, and a Bible

I have three things with me, boys and girls. I have a postcard, a letter, and a Bible. They are different, but they all share some things in common.

A postcard brings a brief message from someone. This postcard is from Aunt Lorraine and tells me that she is having a wonderful time in Florida. It is signed, "Love, Aunt Lorraine."

A letter brings a longer message from someone. This letter is from my friend Bob. It tells me that he has been busy as pastor of a church and hopes that he can stop and see me as he travels through my area this summer. It is signed, "Love, Bob."

The postcard brought a brief message, and the letter brought a longer message.

This third thing I have, the Bible, also brings a message from someone.

There are short books in the Bible; for example, "The Letter of Paul to Titus" is just three chapters, two pages in all; "The Letter of Paul to Philemon" and "The Letter of Jude" are each one chapter, one page in length; "The Second Letter of Peter" is just three chapters, three pages total; and "The Second Letter of John" and "The Third Letter of John" are each just one chapter, one-half page long.

These short books in the Bible are like postcards. They are short messages from God which say that He loves us.

There are also longer books in the Bible; for example, "The Gospel of Matthew" is twenty-eight chapters, thirty-eight pages in all; "The Acts of the Apostles" is also twenty-eight chapters, thirty-seven pages long; "The Gospel of Luke" is twenty-four chapters, thirty-eight pages in all; and "The Letter of Paul to the Romans" is sixteen chapters, seventeen pages long.

These longer books in the Bible are like letters, longer messages from God which say that God loves us.

Whether we get a postcard or a letter in the mail, what's important is that we've heard from someone who loves us. The same thing is true of the Bible. Whether it is a short message or a long message, what's important is that we've heard from someone who loves us.

In the Bible, God has clearly said to us, "Dear human Family, I love you!" [Signed] God.

Prayer:

> Eternal and ever-loving God, thank you for telling us how you feel about us. Through the Creation, you have shown us your majesty and your loving care. By the prophets, you sent your Word to correct us; through Jesus you became the living Word which saved us; and through your apostle Paul you sent your Word to teach us. We are grateful you have spoken to us, and that what you have said is you love us. In the name of Jesus, who is the Word become flesh, we pray. Amen.

SS2824

Seat Belt Safety

Prop: A seat belt (or a picture of one)

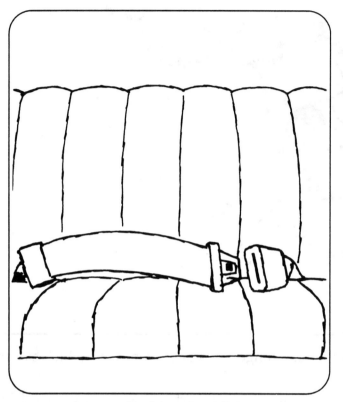

How many of you use a seat belt when you ride in the car? (Encourage the children to respond.) Good! It's very important that you buckle your seat belt when you are traveling in an auto, and it's the law!

Seat belts are very important because they protect us in case of a sudden stop or an accident. Because they hold us securely back in our seats, they keep us safe.

God's commandments also "hold us back" and keep us safe. People who tell lies get into trouble. People who steal get caught. People who are unkind don't have any friends. People who are proud and conceited find that others stay away from them.

If we obey God's commandments, we won't tell lies or steal or be hateful. His commandments "hold us back" from doing such things. They keep us safe–safe in doing what is good and right, safe in doing what pleases God.

Prayer:

Righteous and everlasting God, thank you for giving us rules that will help us do what is good for others and for us. We are also thankful you are a loving God who forgives us our sins and shortcomings. Help us to obey your commandments and, by so doing, to be safe. In Jesus' name. Amen.

The Race

Prop: A "tape" or string to represent a "finish line"

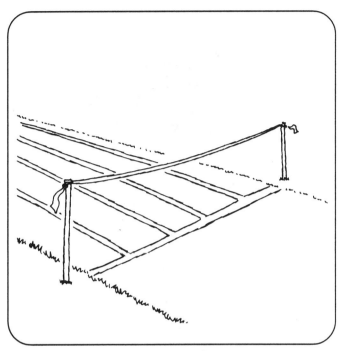

I have with me something which is very important in a race. (Hold up the tape or string.) For what do you think this is used? (Encourage answers from the children.) That was a difficult question. Perhaps I can help a little. This tape (or string) is stretched across the place where the race will end. The winner of the race will run through the tape (or string), either breaking it or pulling it down. The tape (or string) marks the "finish line." (Ask for a couple of volunteers to hold the tape (or string), and then have one or two other children run through it as though they were winning a race.)

The Apostle Paul talks about a race and a finish line in Philippians 3:12-14. Paul pictures himself as a runner who is trying step-by-step to know Jesus better. He is straining toward his goal of completely knowing Jesus, but he has not yet reached that goal. He is somewhere between starting the race and finishing the race.

He will not give up. He goes ahead, always stretching toward the finish line. He wants to be like Jesus and live for Him. Paul says he will not be satisfied until he finishes the race.

You and I are also running a race, stretching toward the finish line. We are trying to be the best people we can be for Jesus. We want to be kinder, more loving, gentler, and more giving. The Holy Spirit encourages us and strengthens us in the race, so when we become tired or are tempted to give up, we can rely on His presence and power.

Prayer:

Father, thank you for the opportunity we have as Christians to know Jesus more fully and to learn more from Him. We want to be better disciples, and we want to live more like Him. Strengthen us and help us run the race to the finish line. In Jesus' name. Amen.

What Our Hands Are Doing

Prop: A large clock

We know what time it is by what the hands of a clock do. (Take time to illustrate this to the children, making sure to explain what the "hands" are and to demonstrate various times on the clock.)

We know what a person is like by what his hands do. A person is helpful if his hands are picking up toys and putting them where they belong. A person is kind if she is doing nice things for others.

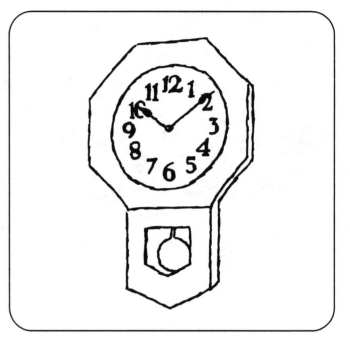

A person is messy if he is throwing things around the room or the house. A person is unkind if she uses her hands to hit others.

We know what time it is by what the clock's hands are doing. Other people know what *we* are like by what *our* hands are doing.

Prayer:

    Creator God, our hands can represent friendship, kindness, and concern, or anger, hostility, and unconcern. Forgive us when our hands do not point to our commitment to Christ. Help us to show our Christian faith in everything we do. These things we pray, remembering that Jesus used his hands for doing good. Amen.

It's Okay to Be Different

Prop: Several wooden building blocks of various sizes and colors, with different letters of the alphabet on them.

How many of you have ever played with blocks like these? (Encourage children to answer by raising their hands.) Only a few/Several/A lot of you have! Let's look at these blocks more closely.

How are these blocks the same? (Encourage responses.) They are all made of wood. They all have letters on them, and they are all the same shape.

How are the blocks different? (Encourage responses.) They have different colors on them. They have different letters on them. They are different sizes.

All of these blocks have some things that are the same and some things that are different. Each block is like the others and unlike the others.

It's the same for you and me, girls and boys. Each of us is somewhat like other people: we have brains; we breathe air; we have skin; we like ice cream.

Each of us is also different from other people: we are different sizes; we have a certain color of skin, a certain complexion, a certain color of hair, a certain color of eyes; and we like different flavors of ice cream.

It's okay to be different! No one else is exactly like you; you're one of a kind, and God loves you just the way you are.

Prayer:

Lord God, Creator of the world and people, thank you that you love us for ourselves and that it's okay for each person to be himself or herself. Help us to appreciate other people, no matter how different they are. In Jesus' name we pray. Amen.

Heavenly Line

Prop: A telephone

We use a telephone to talk to people who are special. How many of you enjoy talking to Grandma or Grandpa or a friend on the phone? (Encourage responses.) We can tell people how we're doing, and ask how they're doing; we can ask them to do something for us, or we can promise to do something for them. A telephone is a great way to stay in touch.

Prayer is also a great way to stay in touch. Through prayer, we stay in touch with God. Prayer is like speaking on the phone to someone special. We can tell God how we're doing, thank Him for what He is doing, ask Him for help with something, or promise to do something for Him. Praying is talking to God. We can talk to Him like we talk to someone special on the telephone.

Prayer:

God who pays attention to us, we give you our thanks and praise that you long for conversation with us and listen to us. We ask for your forgiveness for those times when we have prayed selfishly, thinking only of ourselves. Help us to ask for the right things. We pray in Jesus' name. Amen.

Working Together

Prop: A volleyball

Boys and girls, I have brought something with me which you may recognize. What kind of ball is this? (Encourage responses from the children.) This is a volleyball, and it is used to play an exciting game.

Have you ever watched a volleyball match? (Ask for a show of hands.) A volleyball match is fun to see and to play. When we watch a volleyball match, one thing we notice is that one player cannot play the game all by himself. One person could never cover all the space on one side of the net. One person could not serve the ball, set it up, spike it over the net to the other team's side, and do everything else in a game. That's why several people are needed to play volleyball. It is a team sport.

Our Christian faith is also a team effort. One person cannot do it or live it all by himself. Problems in the world cannot be successfully tackled by only one person; it takes people working together to try to solve them. The ministry of the church cannot be carried out by only one person; we need each other to accomplish things for God's Kingdom. Personal problems cannot always be solved by the individual who has them; oftentimes we need other people to help us. Every Christian needs other people to help, support, encourage, and strengthen him.

Volleyball is a team sport that requires people working together, and so is the Christian faith!

Prayer:

Creator God, who made the world and all that is in it, thank you for giving us the gift of life. Thank you for the opportunity we have to work together to make the world a better place. Forgive us for trying unsuccessfully to "go it alone." Help us join together with other Christians to do your will. In Jesus' name we pray. Amen.

Starting the Tape Over Again

Prop: A portable tape recorder

(Beforehand, tape-record part of a worship service, a conversation, or children at play.)

I have a tape recorder with me today. A tape recorder is an interesting machine; when it's turned on, it "hears" sounds and then preserves them on tape. Let me show you what I mean. (Play what has already been recorded.)

If I want to get rid of what's been recorded, I rewind the tape, start it over again, and record. (If time permits, demonstrate this by recording the children and then playing it back.)

A tape recorder is like God's forgiveness. When we do something we shouldn't, we know we have done wrong, and God knows, too.

When we ask for God's forgiveness, it is as if God "rewinds the tape" and gives us a chance to start all over again. Isn't that wonderful? God erases our wrong. We have a fresh start.

Prayer:

Father, thank you for giving us second chances. You have said that if we are truly sorry for what we have done, and ask you for forgiveness, you will "erase the tape" and remember our sins no more. Help us be more obedient in the future. In the name of Him who came to take our sins away, Jesus Christ, our Lord and Savior. Amen.

It Takes Practice

Prop: A tennis shoe

Boys and girls, if I put on this tennis shoe, what would I need to do to it before I could go play safely? (Let children answer.) I would need to tie the laces first.

How many of you can tie your shoes? (Encourage a show of hands.) Do you remember how you learned to tie shoes? (Encourage responses: "My mother taught me; My father showed me how to do it; It took a long time for me to be able to do it.") Did you tie your shoes correctly the first time you tried? (Encourage responses.) Let me show you how to tie the shoelaces of this tennis shoe. (Demonstrate.) It takes a lot of practice before you are able to do it right. Many things that we want to do well in life require a lot of practice!

Being a good Christian also takes a lot of practice. We may not do everything right the first time. We may have to try over and over again to think of others instead of thinking only of ourselves. We have to practice time and time again to share rather than keep everything for ourselves. We have to try many times to be kind, to forgive, and to accept others who are different, instead of being friends only with those who are like us.

It takes practice to be a good Christian, girls and boys, but God is always encouraging us and loving us. He is always patient with us!

Prayer:

Patient and loving God, we want to be good Christians. We want to be people who live the Christian life well. Help us to keep at it and to practice doing what pleases you. In Jesus' name. Amen.

Belts and Friends

Prop: A belt from a pair of pants or a dress

I've brought a belt with me today, girls and boys. What do we use belts for? (Encourage responses from the children.) We use belts to hold up our pants and to help dresses fit better.

As a person grows older, he may let out his belt several notches to form a bigger circle to fit around him. (Have some fun with this by trying the belt around children.)

Also, as we grow older, each of us enjoys a bigger circle of friends. We meet new people, adding to the group of people we already know, so our circle of friends gets bigger, too.

Of course, a belt is only a certain length; it makes only so big a circle. If we grow too big for the belt, we have to get a bigger one.

It is different concerning our friends. No matter how big our circle of friends gets, there's always room for more. No matter how many people we know, we can continue to make our circle of friends even bigger.

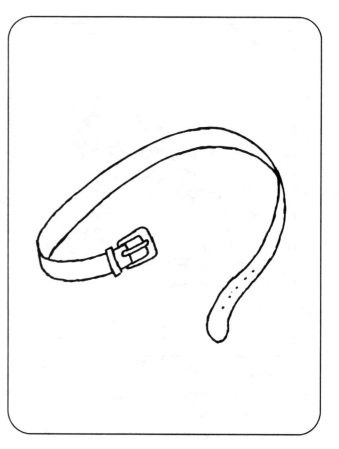

Prayer:

Creator and faithful Friend, we give you thanks for your friendship and for the friendship of others. We know how important friends are, for they pick us up when we are "down" and celebrate with us when we are "up." Forgive us for making our circle too small or unchanging. Thank you for sending Jesus as a friend of sinners. We ask it in His name. Amen.

Whistling Teakettle

Prop: A whistling teakettle

Today I have something with me from my kitchen, girls and boys. This is a teakettle. What sound does this teakettle make when the water is boiling? (Encourage responses, such as whistles.) Wow! What great teakettle noises you make!

We know the water is boiling when the teakettle whistles and makes its noise. We know dinner is ready when Dad or Mom announces, "Dinnertime!" We know the family is ready to go for a drive when everyone is seated in the car and all seat belts are fastened. All these things are "signs of readiness."

Christians should show "signs of readiness" to live for God. What kinds of actions show people that you are ready to live for God? (Let the children share ideas, such as kindness, helpfulness, patience, not going along with the crowd when they do wrong.) Here are some other ways to show people that you are ready to live for God. (Read Ephesians 4:29-32.)

Remember, just as the teakettle's whistle tells you the water is boiling and ready to use, your actions can tell other people that you are ready to live for God in every part of your life.

Prayer:

Father, we want to live for you, and we want other people to know it. Help us to show our readiness to live for you in our everyday actions. In Jesus' name. Amen.

SS2824

Measuring Up

Prop: A cloth tape measure

Girls and boys, what is this? (Encourage answers from the children.) I have a tape measure. We can use this to see how big something is.

Let's measure how tall you are. (Select a child and measure his height.) Let's measure what size your feet are. (Measure another child's feet.) Let's measure your waist. (Measure a child's waist.).This tape measure is very helpful!

It can show how much you've grown. I bet you've become taller in the last year; your feet are probably bigger; there are more inches around your waist than before. The tape measure tells us how much you have grown physically.

Boys and girls, there is also a kind of tape measure that shows how much we have

grown spiritually: it's the Bible. The Bible tells us to treat others the way we want to be treated, to love God and other people, to be patient with people and go the extra mile, and to forgive people when they have wronged us. Using the Bible as our tape measure, we can see how much we've grown as Christians. Hopefully, in the last year we've become kinder, more patient, and more forgiving.

Of course, God is helping us grow physically and spiritually. He wants us to grow to be the best we can be. The best way we can say "Thank you" to God is to try to measure up to what we know He wants.

Prayer:

God, we give you thanks for the way you care about us and want what's best for us. Help us to be the kind of people you want us to be. We truly want to measure up. In the name of Jesus, we pray. Amen.

Seeing Clearly

Prop: A pair of eyeglasses

I'm wearing something which helps me to see better. Do you know what it is? (Encourage responses.) It's a pair of eyeglasses. They help me see you and everyone and everything here clearly. If I take them off, everything would look blurry.

Even better than eyeglasses, Jesus helps us see better and more clearly. Sometimes if we're not careful, we may think that keeping all our toys to ourselves, rather than sharing them with others, is the way to be; that hitting people when we're angry at them, rather than talking to them, is how we should act; that taking something we want that belongs to someone else, rather than asking to borrow it, is the way to get what we want. We all know that's not the way to be, but that is how we somethimes "see" things.

When I hear the stories of Jesus and learn how He lived, it helps me to see clearly how I should live. Jesus, even better than eyeglasses, helps me to see more clearly.

Prayer:

Almighty God, we give you thanks for life and for the relationships we have with others. We give you the greatest thanks of all for Jesus, in whose light we see life clearly. Amen.

SS2824

Long-Lasting Flavor

Prop: A pack of chewing gum

What do I have here? (Encourage answers.) How many of you enjoy chewing gum? (Encourage a show-of-hands response.) I enjoy chewing gum: it tastes good, and it seems to relax me.

I've noticed, though, that after awhile, the gum loses its flavor. It just doesn't taste as good anymore. It's time to throw it away and replace it with another stick.

Boys and girls, being a Christian is *not* like chewing a stick of gum–the flavor *never* wears out. No matter how long we have followed Jesus Christ–a little while or a long while–it stays good. The happiness we have learning more about Jesus, telling people about Him, and trying to live like Him never goes away.

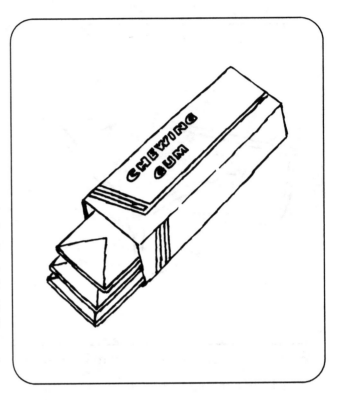

Prayer:

Gracious God, in following Jesus we have learned the truth about life and enjoyed great happiness. Thank you for Jesus. Forgive us for those times when we have wondered if it was really worth it. Remind us frequently that the Christian life never loses its flavor. In the name of Him who came that we might have life and have it abundantly, Jesus of Nazareth. Amen.

SS2824

Junk

Props: Some "junk" items from the garage or attic placed in a wagon or in some sort of other moveable container

Look at what I have with me! (Pull wagon amidst the children.) I brought a lot of junk to share with you. Let's see what I have in my "junk wagon." (Mention items.) I have a rusty wrench, an old bird cage, a chipped set of orange juice glasses with "Visit Florida, the Sunshine State" on them, a tattered jacket, a baseball glove that has seen better days, a radio which may or may not work, a pair of silver-colored women's shoes, etc.

I have a lot of things here, boys and girls, but I don't think it's worth very much. The wrench is rusty; the bird cage is old and beat-up; the orange juice glasses should be thrown away; the jacket doesn't look good and would not keep a person very warm; the baseball glove would not help much in catching a baseball; the radio probably doesn't work; I don't know where or when someone would wear those shoes. Maybe someone would buy all these items for a few dollars, or maybe not. This junk is just not very valuable.

Sometimes we may feel like junk. We make mistakes; we don't do things the correct way; we forget what we should remember; we don't always treat others the way we should; we may be sloppy; we get angry over nothing; we let things slide by which should be resisted or at least challenged. Many of us have times when we don't feel worth very much.

We need to remember God made us in His image (Genesis 1:27 and Psalm 8). He created us with tremendous potential. When we allow God to work in our lives, He "redoes" us and helps us be the best we can be.

At times we may feel like worthless junk; but since God loves us, we are valuable. He can make something better out of us.

Prayer:

Lord God, the Creator of us all, we give you thanks for making and loving us. We know we are valuable to you. Lift us up and help us to think better of ourselves and do what will glorify your holy name. These things we pray in Jesus' name. Amen.

SS2824

Fruit of the Vine

Prop: A bowl of real grapes (or some other fruit) and a bowl of artificial ones

Girls and boys, I have brought with me two bunches of grapes. These grapes may look alike, but they are not really the same. Let's look more carefully at them. (With the children examine the genuine and artificial grapes.)

I think that we would all agree that one bowl of grapes is real and the other one is not. These grapes (hold up) are artificial or fake, and these other grapes (hold up) are genuine or real.

Boys and girls, sometimes people may look alike, but they may not really be the same. Some people may appear to be kind or loving, but they are actually unkind or unloving. Some people may appear to be generous or humble or accepting, but in fact they are stingy, prideful, and judgmental.

We needed to take a close look at the grapes to discover which ones were real and which were not. We had to "get to know" them in order to make a decision about them. We need to take a close look at people to find out who is "real" and who is not. We have to get to know people before we can make decisions about them.

Prayer:

Loving and knowing God, you see into our hearts and know who is truly kind and loving, and who is not. Help us not to make our decisions about people based on appearance, but to look more closely by getting to know them. Whether they are real or fake, help us to love them. These things we pray in the name of Jesus, who never faked love, but really cared for every person. Amen.

SS2824

Getting Ready

Prop: A portable alarm clock

I've brought an alarm clock with me, boys and girls. If I wanted to get up at 7:00 in the morning, how would I set the clock? (Encourage answers from the children.) I would set the alarm by twisting this stem on the back of the clock until the indicator was at 7:00. Then I would pull out this other stem so the alarm would go off at the proper time. The alarm would let me know when it is time to get out of bed and get ready for the day. (If time permits, move the hands to set the time so the alarm will sound. If I did not have this alarm clock, I might keep sleeping and miss getting up when I should.

Girls and boys, the Advent season is like an alarm clock for Christians. Advent begins four Sundays before Christmas and continues until Christmas Eve. Advent "wakes us up" and lets us know that Christmas will be coming soon. It helps us get ready to celebrate Christmas.

Getting ready means writing Christmas lists, choosing gifts for loved ones, buying and decorating a Christmas tree, and reminding ourselves that because God loves us, He sent Jesus to Earth. But Advent is more than this. It also reminds us that God continues to love us and wants us to love each other and give to each other.

Getting ready for Christmas means doing important, special things. Advent helps us remember to do those things. It is like an alarm ringing. It calls out, "Christmas is coming. Wake up. Don't sleep. Don't miss it. Get ready!"

Prayer:

God, who sent Jesus, we thank you, and we praise your name for all good gifts but especially for the gift of Jesus. Help us to be "awake" this Christmas season and to get ready for the celebration of Jesus' birth. We ask it in His name. Amen.

SS2824

A Power to Help

Prop: A jar of peanut butter

(To the children) How many of you enjoy peanut butter sandwiches? (Encourage a show of hands.) I will just take off this lid, and you'll be able to see and to smell this delicious peanut butter. (Pretend to have great difficulty in removing the lid.) There's something the matter here! I can't seem to remove the lid. It's on too tight.

Will someone help me? (Invite one or more children, depending on time available, to assist in removing the lid.) There, the lid's off. I needed some additional strength to be able to get the peanut butter jar open. I needed to get help, didn't I?

Boys and girls, what does God expect from us? (Encourage answers.) God wants us to be nice, not naughty; God tells us to share, not to keep everything for ourselves; He expects us to love difficult people, not to hate them. God expects a lot from us! If we had to do these things on our own, we would never be able to get them done. We are just not strong enough! We would have just as much trouble as I had with the peanut butter jar!

Fortunately, God gives us His power to be able to do what He asks of us. He is willing to fill us with His Spirit so that we are able to be nice, to share, and to love even difficult people. All that we need to do is ask for God's help and be open to His Spirit. I asked you for help with the peanut butter jar lid. Are you willing to ask God for help?

The next time you eat a peanut butter sandwich, remember that God is always present and available to help us if we ask Him.

Prayer:

God of power and love, thank you that through your love you sent Jesus to help and to save us in our greatest need. We are thankful, too, that when we find ourselves "up against it," we can count on you to give us strength. We want to be your obedient children, so be with us and strengthen us to do your will. We ask it in Jesus' name. Amen.

SS2824

God's Love Never Runs Out

Prop: A box of pop-up facial tissues

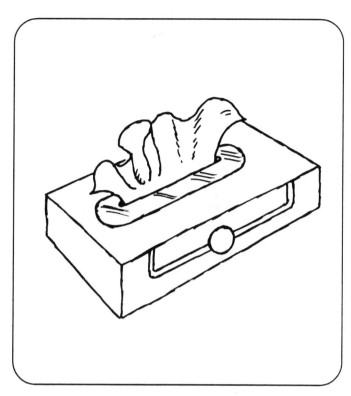

Girls and boys, look at this box of tissues. There's something very interesting about it. When I remove a tissue (do so), another tissue pops up to take its place. Would you like to try it? (Invite several children to take tissues, thus revealing more.) It appears that we won't run out of tissues, for there's always more to come!

It's the same way with God's love, boys and girls. No matter how much love God gives to us, He always has more to share. God cares about you, wants the very best for you, and wants to help you.

Of course, at some point this tissue box will run out of tissues. There are only so many of them inside, but God's love will never run out. There's always more to come!

Prayer:

God of love, we give you thanks for the never-ending way you care about us. Help us to care more about other people. We ask this in Jesus' name. Amen.

SS2824

Brought Together

Prop: A hair ribbon or an elastic hair band

I have with me something which some of the girls in our group may have worn, but which the boys have not. What is this? (Show the object to the children and encourage them to respond.) A hair ribbon or an elastic hair band holds to-gether a bunch of hair. It brings many strands of hair together and holds them in one place.

The church is filled with different kinds of people–women, men, children; people with light skin, dark skin, and yellow skin; younger people and older people; Americans, Europeans, Latin Americans, and Chinese; tall folks and short folks; thin ones and stocky ones, to mention just some of them.

There are many different kinds of people in the church, but Jesus holds all of them together. He brings Christians into one body called the church. "There is neither Jew nor Greek, slave nor free, male nor female, for you are all one in Christ Jesus" (Galatians 3:28).

Prayer:

    Lord God, thank you that Jesus is the foundation of our faith, for in Him we are all drawn together as one. Forgive us when we act as if differences really counted more than our union and equality in Christ. We ask it in the name of Him who makes us one body, Jesus Christ our Lord and Savior. Amen.

SS2824

I Can Do It! (Not Really)

Prop: A guitar (or other instrument) on which one has no proficiency at all

I would like to play a song for you on this guitar. Somebody asked me if I would, and I said, "I can do it!" Let me share this tune with you. (Pretend to play a serious tune, obviously doing a very poor job of it.)

Girls and boys, I don't know what is the matter! I said I could play and that I would play, so let me try that again. (Play again with blatant deficiencies.)

What's gone wrong? I thought I could play the guitar. I told other people I could play the guitar. I told you I would share a tune with you.

I guess if I had stopped to think about it seriously, I would have realized that I really cannot play the guitar. I've never played one before. I've never taken a single lesson; I've never practiced. I was fooling myself and others when I said I could do it.

Jesus' disciples sometimes overestimated their ability to do what Jesus taught them and to be the kind of disciples Jesus wanted. *Overestimated* is a word which means that they thought they could do more than they really could. Jesus warned them that leading the kind of life he set before them would not be easy.

Sometimes we may think that being a Christian is easy. Perhaps we think we can do it with little trouble and without any help. When we are honest with ourselves, we realize that leading a Christian life takes a lot of work. It is only through Jesus' example, the power of the Holy Spirit, and the guidance of God that we can get better at it.

We are fooling ourselves and others when we say, "We can do it!" Of course, we are not fooling God. God knows our shortcomings, our weaknesses, and our wishful thinking. The great thing is, boys and girls, that God *can* do it! Let's trust Him to help us.

Prayer:

God, who gets the job done, we give you thanks that you do not give up on us when we think too much or too little of ourselves. Teach us humility and lead us in the paths of righteousness for your name's sake. Amen.

Accepted Just as We Are

Prop: A pair of binoculars

Boys and girls, have you ever seen these before? They are binoculars. You look in the small end, and it makes something way over there seem very close and very big. If you look in the big end, it makes something close seem like it's far away and very small. (Demonstrate this, letting some children look for themselves.)

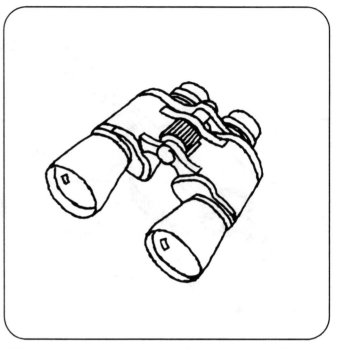

These binoculars remind us of something Jesus once said. He told us not to see all the bad things about other people and refuse to see the things that are wrong with us. It's like looking through the binoculars. Do we look through the small end of our binoculars at other people, making their faults look bigger than they are? Do we see our own faults as smaller than they are?

We need to look at others as they really are. We need to look at ourselves as we really are. None of us is all bad or all good. God loves us, and He forgives and accepts us just as we are.

Prayer:

Gracious God, you see us just as we are. You know how unloving and unlovable we can be, and yet you love us. Thank you for accepting us and loving us as we are. Help us to be more patient and less judgmental of other people. In Jesus' name we pray. Amen.

SS2824

Light

Prop: A flashlight

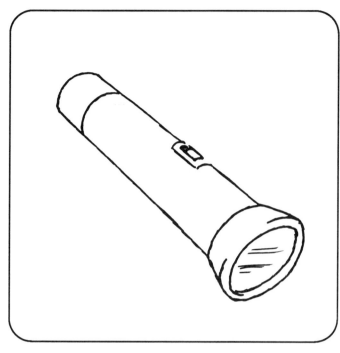

I have something which you will probably recognize. It's something that you'll find lying around your home or perhaps in the trunk of the family car. What is it? (Encourage children to respond and to indicate whether or not, and where, there are flashlights in their homes or in their families' cars.)

Flashlights are very helpful; they allow us to see in the dark. Sometimes we are afraid of the dark because we can't see what's there. We may see shapes, but we aren't sure what they are. With the flashlight, we can see clearly to find a safe path. The light shows us objects which were only shapes in the dark. We become comfortable because we know what's truly there.

Jesus is the light of the world (John 8:12). He shows us the truth about life. He helps us find a path through life because he shows us the way things are and what is really there.

Jesus teaches us that it is better to give than to receive, that loving God and loving those around us are the most important rules, that thinking about others as well as ourselves is the right thing to do. He tells us that being selfish and being concerned only about ourselves is not the way to be. Instead, selfishness is an obstacle to being happy.

Jesus is like a flashlight–the light of the world. In Jesus' light, we see what life is really all about.

Prayer:

Eternal and ever-present God, you began your great act of Creation by causing the light to shine. Later you sent Jesus, the Light of the World, to give us light in the darkness of our sin. Come more fully into our lives and give us your light. In Jesus' name we pray. Amen.

SS2824

Going Through the Motions

Prop: A windshield wiper blade

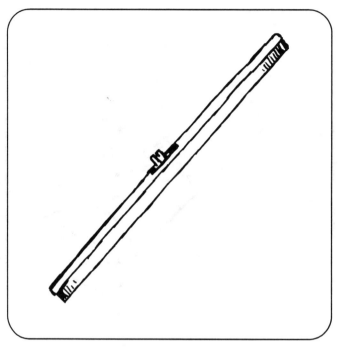

This is an unusual object! Does anyone know what it is? (Encourage responses.) Let me give you a hint: it is something that you find on all cars, trucks, and busses. You find it near or on the wind-shields. (Encourage children to guess.) It is something that helps the driver to see. It keeps the rain and the snow off the windshield. It is a wind-shield wiper blade!

This windshield wiper blade is very important. Without it, the driver of the car or truck or bus could not see through the windshield on a rainy or snowy day. The windshield wiper goes back and forth, back and forth, to whisk off the raindrops or the snowflakes. (With the wiper blade, demonstrate the motion for the children.) The purpose of the windshield wiper blade is to keep the windshield clean.

Christians are somewhat like windshield wiper blades. They are busy going to church, going to Sunday School, reading the Bible, attending meetings, helping others, and trying to be kind. There's a lot of back and forth motion with Christians–back and forth to church, in and out of Sunday School, opening and closing the Bible, going from this meeting to that one, helping one person and then another, being kind to a neighbor and perhaps a stranger.

Christians do these things because they want to grow in their faith, they want to thank God for His good gifts (including Jesus), and they want to lead lives that show to others that God is real and that Jesus' way truly *is* the way to live.

Of course, it is only when their hearts are in all these activities that they count. Otherwise, they are just motions. The purpose of going through the motions for a wiper blade is to keep the windshield clear and clean. The purpose of going through the motions for a Christian is to serve.

Prayer:

    Lord God, from the very beginning you have been active in the world you have created–doing good, granting forgiveness, bringing order out of disorder, and working for peace. Thank you for all you do. Help us to be active in the world, serving you. In Jesus' name. Amen.

Identifying Christians

Prop: A police officer's badge

Girls and boys, I am holding something which you may recognize. What is this? (Point to the badge.) It is a police officer's badge.

We can recognize a police officer by the badge that he or she wears. When we see that badge, we know that person is someone who upholds the law, someone who can protect us or help us.

How can we recognize who is a Christian? (Encourage answers from the children.) We can tell who is a Christian by how he or she acts. Does that person love, forgive, show kindness, and practice honesty?

Girls and boys, we can recognize a Christian by the "badge" of his or her actions.

Prayer:

Almighty God, who sent your Son to live among us and to redeem us, we give you thanks that we may choose to follow Jesus. Help us be the kind of Christians Jesus wants us to be–loving, forgiving, kind, and honest. May we show that we are Christians by the way we act. In Jesus' name. Amen.

Shining Star Publications, Copyright © 1992, A Division of Good Apple

SS2824

Mileage Markers

Prop: A couple of cardboard signs modelled after highway mileage markers

I brought some signs with me; let's read these signs together? (Call on children to read the signs aloud.) This sign says "Greenfield 20 (miles)," the second one says "Richmond 100 (miles)." They mean that we must go forward 20 miles in order to reach Greenfield, and we must go ahead 100 miles to arrive at Richmond.

These highway signs are very helpful to us: they tell us where we are and how close we are to where we want to go. By looking at the mileage markers on the highway, we know how far we still have to go to reach our destination. (Point to signs.) If we are driving toward Greenfield, we still have 20 miles to go; if we are headed toward Richmond, we still have 100 miles to drive.

In the Bible we find some rules which act as "mileage markers" for Christians. These rules allow us to see where we are

on our Christian journey and how far we still have to go to be obedient to God and lead lives that please Him. The Old Testament tells us not to desire what other people have (Deuteronomy 5:21). It tells us not to steal (Deuteronomy 5:19). The Old Testament tells us to honor and respect our parents (Deuteronomy 5:16).

In the New Testament, Jesus tells us to treat others as we would like them to treat us (Matthew 7:12). He also tells us to go the second mile (Matthew 5:41) and to forgive as often as necessary (Matthew 18:21-22). He tells us to love the Lord our God with all our heart and with all our soul and with all our mind and to love our neighbors as ourselves" (Matthew 22:37-39).

Some Christians may be doing quite well with these rules. Though they have not "arrived," they have come a long way toward full obedience to God. Others may have farther to go on their obedience "journey."

Shining Star Publications. Copyright © 1992, A Division of Good Apple

SS2824

Mileage markers help us on the highways. Biblical rules help us on our Christian journeys.

If we have a car breakdown on the highway, a highway patrolman or an auto mechanic will help us. If we have a spiritual breakdown on our Christian journey, God is there to help us (and to forgive us).

Prayer:

God and Father of our Lord Jesus Christ, we give you thanks and praise for creating us, encouraging us, giving us rules by which to live, and forgiving us when we are sorry for not living in obedience to those rules. Help us to live more fully and more obediently according to your commandments. In Jesus' name we pray. Amen.

SS2824

Garbage in Life

Prop: A bag of garbage

What do I have with me? (Encourage responses from the children.) I have a bag full of garbage!

Who takes out the garbage in your house? (Encourage answers.) Do you help some by gathering things from your room to put in the garbage?

Here is some garbage from my house. Let's see what I have–a banana peel, some cellophane, some torn-in-half envelopes, some empty yogurt containers, a saltine cracker box, and some paper towels. I wouldn't want these things lying around my home; they would be messy and smelly, so I collected them and will put them out in the trash. Then my house will be cleaned-up and garbage-free.

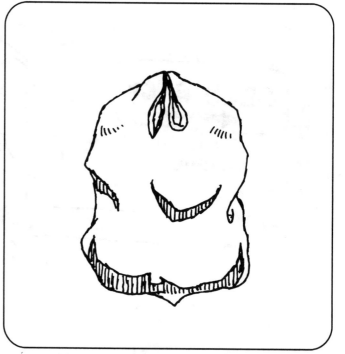

In a way, I suppose, all of us have some "garbage" in our lives–things we have done we wish we hadn't, things we didn't do that we wish we had, cruel words we have spoken, anger, and resentment. This "garbage" threatens to mess up our lives. We desperately need someone to collect our "garbage" and throw it out, but it will take a special person to do this. We can't do it by ourselves.

Jesus is the one who can get rid of our "garbage." He has the power and the love to collect all the things messing up our lives and take them away. All that we need to do is ask Jesus for help and trust Him to respond.

Prayer:

Almighty and everlasting God, you sent Jesus into the world to save us from our sins and to clean up our lives. We are confident that no piece of "garbage" is too large for Him to remove. Thank you for your cleansing power in Jesus Christ! Amen.

Behavior Thermometer

Prop: An oral thermometer

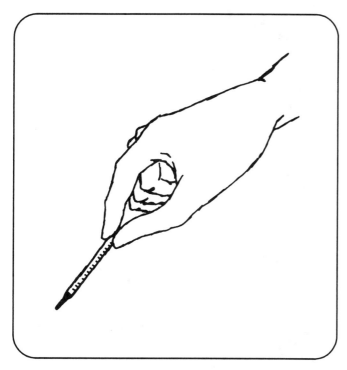

I have something very small with me, but this "something" is very important. (Hold up the thermometer for all to see.) What is this? (Encourage the children to answer.) It is a thermometer.

A thermometer helps us know when a person is sick. By placing this in someone's mouth, we can know if that person has a fever. (If sufficient time is available, put a thermometer in a volunteer's mouth; then read it.) The thermometer tells us a person's temperature.

What is a "normal temperature"? It is 98.6 degrees Fahrenheit. If a person's temperature is above this, that person is sick. If a person's temperature is below this, it can also mean that person is not feeling well.

The way people treat each other is a "thermometer" of "spiritual health." If a person is cheerful and kind to others, he is probably doing just fine! If a person is unkind and unloving to other people, it may show that he is "spiritually sick."

When the "thermometer" says that a person is "spiritually sick," we must try to help him. God is involved in the healing process, and you and I can be involved, too. What can we do? (If there is time, encourage the children to share ideas.) We can try to be nice to that person by saying a kind word or doing something nice. We can encourage others to act in the same loving way to him. We can pray for God's help. We can talk about the situation with our parents, our church leaders, or our Sunday School teacher.

Let's pay attention to the way people treat each other because people's actions are a thermometer that tells us if they are "spiritually well" or "sick."

Prayer:

Father, thank you that you made us for relationships with each other. We know that we need one another! We also know that people do not always treat others in the "healthiest" of ways. Help us to recognize this and respond with love, prayer, and helpful attention. We know that you are the great Physician, who can bring health and wholeness. We ask these things in the name of Jesus, who went about healing. Amen.

Putting On the Armor

Prop: A football helmet

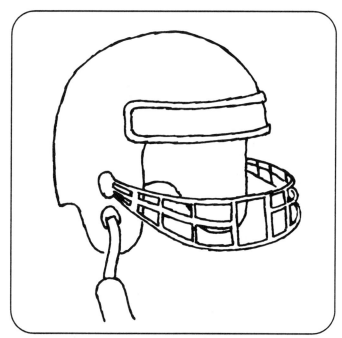

What is this? (Hold up the helmet.) It is a football helmet.

Football players wear football helmets like this one as part of their uniform. The football helmet is designed to protect their heads and keep them from being injured. (If possible, put on the helmet to show how it fits.)

Ephesians 6:10-17 tells us that Christians are to put on the armor of God. His "armor" helps us protect ourselves from the values of the world, which are different from God's values. The world teaches selfishness; God teaches sharing. The world teaches hate; God teaches love. The world teaches dishonesty; God teaches honesty. The world teaches thinking only of yourself; God teaches thinking of others. The world teaches bragging; God teaches humility. The world teaches war; God teaches peace.

As a football helmet protects the player from physical injury, so "God's armor" protects the Christian from spiritual injury. God wants us to put on the "breastplate of righteousness" to help us be good (moral), not bad (immoral). The world tempts us to do wrong and try to get away with it; God teaches us to do good.

Let's put on God's armor so we can lead the kind of lives that show God's love and grace.

Prayer:

Gracious and loving God, thank you for giving us a way of life that makes us truly happy and lets others know that we are your people. Thank you, too, for showing us your way, through the life, death, and resurrection of Jesus. Help us to put on your armor to protect us from temptation. We ask it in the name of Jesus, who was tempted in the wilderness but was victorious. Amen.

Why We Give Gifts

Prop: A birthday or Christmas present, a bouquet of flowers, or some other gift

Boys and girls, I have brought a present with me this morning. I am going to give this gift to a friend. How do you think it will make my friend feel? (Invite the children to share their answers to the question.) This gift should make my friend very happy. One reason we give gifts to people is because we want to make them happy. We want to make them happy because we love them.

We give gifts for another reason, too, girls and boys. We give gifts to each other because God gave to us the gift of his Son, Jesus. That gift has made us very happy.

When you give a gift or receive one, remember that the gift carries love with it and brings happiness. It reminds us of God's gift to us, Jesus, sent in love to bring happiness into our lives.

Prayer:

Gracious God, thank you for all the good gifts of life. Most of all, we thank you for the greatest gift, your Son, Jesus Christ. Help us to spread love and happiness to others. In Jesus' name we pray. Amen.

SS2824

Speed Limit

Prop: A replica of a speed limit sign, with 55 mph on it

Have you ever seen one of these? (Hold up speed limit sign.) Where did you see it? (Let children answer: on the way to Grandma and Grandpa's, on the highway, on the road while on vacation, while riding with Mom and Dad.)

This tells us how fast we can go. We can go no faster than 55 miles per hour. We can go no faster without endangering our lives or the lives of other people.

Jesus' teachings act as speed limit signs for us. They tell us what the limits are. For example: they tell us that having too many things is beyond Christian limits. Jesus asked, "What good will it be for a man if he gains the whole world, yet forfeits his soul?" (See Matthew 16:26.) It is not good for a person to think material things will bring happiness. Trying to gain many possessions goes beyond the limit for a Christian.

Jesus told of a rich young ruler (Luke 18:18-25) who was a good person but had many possessions. He wanted eternal life, but he could not bring himself to give up what he had and give to the poor. Jesus' point in telling the story was to illustrate that people sometimes go beyond the Christian limits. This rich young ruler had exceeded the limit of what he truly needed. His "wants" were greater than his "needs."

Jesus' limits are for the benefit of others and ourselves. A person who refuses to share not only hurts others, but also hurts himself. A person who is unfeeling toward the needy not only doesn't help them but also doesn't help herself to be truly happy.

Driving beyond the speed limit and going beyond our Christian limits are both dangerous–for others and for ourselves. Let's obey both.

Prayer:

God, who cares about us and who comes to us in every new moment of the day, thank you for setting limits and for having Jesus teach us what those limits are. Help us to go at the proper pace and live in obedience to your rules. We ask it in Jesus' name. Amen.

Don't Fence Me In

Prop: A picture or drawing of a fence

We see fences many places–chain-link fences around playgrounds, wooden fences around homes, iron fences in front yards, and wire fences around farmers' fields. Girls and boys, where was the last fence that you saw? (Encourage the children to recall fences they last saw.)

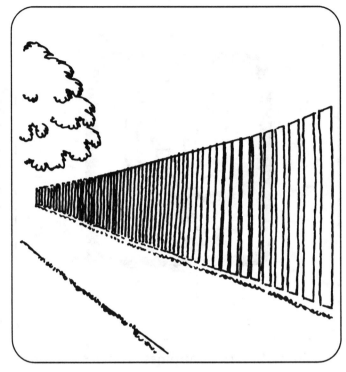

Fences separate sections of land from one another and show us who owns what. This fenced-in property belongs to this person; the land on the other side of the fence belongs to another person. (Illustrate, using the picture or drawing of a fence.)

Sometimes people look at God's love in the same way. They see themselves and their friends and relatives as the only ones included in God's love. They think that God's love stops with them and does not include their neighbors. They think they have God's love all to themselves.

However, God's love has no boundaries. It goes beyond all divisions that *we* create. It extends to all people! In John 3:16 we are told that God so loved the *world* that He gave His only begotten Son . . .

All people are loved by God. His love just cannot be "fenced in."

Prayer:

> Great God, you are the Creator of the whole world, and your love extends to everyone. You sent Jesus for the salvation of the world. Great, loving, and caring God, we give you our thanks and our praise. We do so in Jesus' name. Amen.

SS2824

Front and Back, Inside and Out

Props: Two pieces of wood with the same dimensions, one good and one decayed, but both painted white on one side

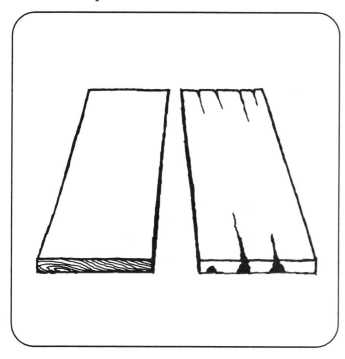

Girls and boys, I have two pieces of wood here. (Show children the two pieces with the painted sides facing them.) They are about the same size, and both are painted white. I guess they are exactly the same.

Wait a second! (Turn both pieces of wood over so that the bare sides are facing the children.) They are not the same! This one is good, sturdy wood; nothing is the matter with it. This one is decayed; it's not very sturdy, so a lot is wrong with it!

Both pieces of wood looked just the same from one side. Both were painted white, but as you can see, they are not the same. On the good piece of wood, the paint makes it look even better. On the decayed piece, the paint hides the decay and makes it look better than it really is.

Jesus accused some people of being "like whitewashed tombs, which look beautiful on the outside but on the inside are full of dead men's bones and everything unclean (Matthew 23:27-28). Jesus was upset with those people because they pretended to be good, and looked good on the outside to others, but inside they were evil.

You and I must be careful not to just *appear* to be good but to really *be* good. As Christians, we should be sincere about the caring things we do and the kind things we say.

We must be careful how we look at other people. What appears "on the outside" could be misleading. We may be tricked by people just as we were almost tricked by the two pieces of wood. We need to look carefully to discover the truth!

Prayer:

Almighty and everlasting God, thank you for creating us with minds to think and eyes to see. Help us, whether we are looking at ourselves or at others, to see the truth. Help us, whether we are thinking about ourselves or thinking about others, to see all sides. In Jesus' name. Amen.

SS2824

Calling Cards

("How Can We Tell Them We Are Christians?")

Prop: A stack of calling cards

Hi, I'm pleased to meet you. I'm Cliff Cain, a professor at Franklin College. (Hand out calling cards to each child and introduce yourself.)

Girls and boys, I have just given you a "calling card." Cards like this are often used by someone, because they tell other people who he/she is. The cards have a person's name and also that person's job on them. By giving people these cards, I am telling them who I am and what I do.

What if I wanted to tell people that I am a Christian? How could I do that?

I could get cards printed that say, "Cliff Cain, Christian," and I could pass them out, but I think there may be a better way! I tell people that I am a *Christian* by the way I act. When I am forgiving, that tells others I am a Christian. When I am loving and kind, my actions tell others that I am a Christian.

How can you tell or show others that you are a Christian? (Encourage the children to suggest a variety of ways .) Those are good ideas! Try to make some of them your "calling cards."

Prayer:

> God of grace, we celebrate the fact that you do kind and loving things for us. Who you are has been revealed through what you do. May it be the same with us, Lord. Help us to show others that we are Christians by what we say and do. In this way, our actions will be our Christian "calling cards." These things we ask in Jesus' name. Amen.

God Made Me Do It

Props: A wooden board with a nail sticking out, and a hammer

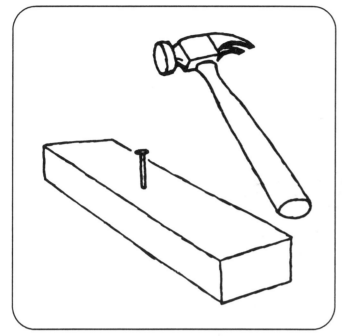

I have some workshop tools with me. What tools do you see? (Encourage children to respond.) Yes, here's a nail; yes, here's a hammer.

I need some volunteers who will hammer the nail a little farther into the board. Who would like to help me? (Depending on time, select an appropriate number of helpers.)

Thank you for doing such a fine job, but I think the nail needs to be hammered just a little bit more. I'll take the hammer and hit the nail. (Strike the nail once or twice and then pretend to hit yourself on the thumb.) Ouch! I hit my thumb. Wow, does that smart!

I don't know why God made me hurt myself! Why did He do that to me? What did I do to deserve that?

(Pause). You know, girls and boys, God didn't make me hurt myself. I caused myself to be hurt; I wasn't careful enough with the hammer. God didn't do that to me; I did it to myself!

Sometimes people blame God for the bad or painful things that happen to them when they actually are the cause. Someone is late for a meeting and blames God when there is no parking space. Someone hurries too fast, falls down, and blames God for the resulting injury. Someone smokes cigarettes and then blames God when he gets lung cancer. Someone is unkind to another person; when that person is unkind in return, God gets blamed.

Boys and girls, God wants only good things for us. He is always working for what's best.

At the same time, God has given us freedom to choose for ourselves. Sometimes we make unwise choices that bring about trouble for us. We can't blame God or anyone else for those bad things that result from our own choices.

We need to use our God-given freedom wisely. In using it wisely we can avoid some bad and painful things. Next time I will be much more careful with the hammer, for I do not choose to hurt myself!

 SS2824

Prayer:

> God, thank you for giving us free choice. You have put us in charge of ourselves. When we make bad choices, we have only ourselves to blame. Forgive us for those times when we have blamed you for our problems when we should have been pointing a finger at ourselves. We know that you want only what is good for us. Give us your insight to help us choose wisely. We praise you as the source of both wisdom and truth. In Jesus' name. Amen.

SS2824

A Story to Remember

Prop: A short piece of string already tied into a small bow

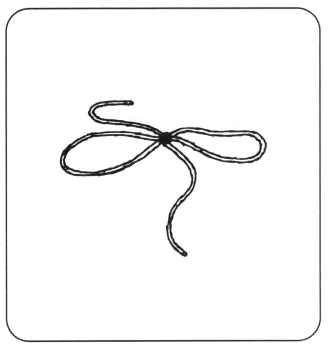

If I want to remember something, what can I do? (Encourage responses from the children.) I can write it down on a piece of paper; I can have someone remind me; I can tie a piece of string on my finger. (Have one of the children help put the string onto your finger.) Now what was it I was going to remember? Oh yes. Someone's birthday is tomorrow, and I wanted to remember to send that person a pretty birthday card. I didn't forget! Do you think the string helped?

One of the last things Jesus did before He was crucified was to eat a special meal with His disciples. He knew the events of the coming hours would confuse them and make them afraid. He wouldn't be with them much longer, and He wanted them to remember all He had taught them. At this "Last Supper," as Jesus and His disciples ate and drank, He told them to do this "in remembrance of me" (1 Corinthians 11:25). After Jesus' death and resurrection, His followers continued to meet together often for this "meal of remembrance."

(Many churches practice communion today. Explain to the children your church's teaching on this topic. Be sure to point out that the reason for it is to help remember what Jesus did for us.)

Prayer:

Eternal God, we give you thanks for the life of Jesus Christ. We marvel at the way He loved all people, and at the way He forgave even those who had mistreated Him. Help us to remember Him, and try to be more like Him. In Jesus' name. Amen.

 SS2824

Bridges

Prop: A picture or a drawing of a bridge over a valley

I have a picture of something you may remember driving on in the family car. What is this? (Show the picture to the children and encourage their responses.) It is a bridge.

This bridge has been built over a valley. It has a strong support structure underneath to keep the bridge from falling. (Point out the support structure in the picture, being sure to emphasize size, strength, and dependability.) The bridge has guardrails on the sides to keep cars from going off the edge. (Point out the guardrails in the picture, emphasizing their importance for safety.)

A bridge allows us to drive over a valley safely; there is the strong support underneath, and there are safety rails on the sides.

Girls and boys, I am sure that most of the time you are quite happy. Life is a lot of fun (as it should be), but sometimes there are moments when you are sad or feeling bad. Grown-ups call these moments of sadness or feeling bad "valleys." "Valleys" are low points; they are times when things are not going right, when our feelings are hurt, and when we just don't feel well.

Fortunately, like bridges, we have a "support system" underneath and "safety rails" on the sides. Our "support system" is God's strength. He picks us up when we are down, and gives us the power to continue. God is dependable, stronger than the pillar-like supports holding up a bridge. (Refer to the picture again.) Our "safety rails" are our friends and loved ones. These are people who care about us and keep us from going "over the edge." They help us with the things that are causing us problems.

You and I can cross our "valleys" like bridges, boys and girls, because we have God's strength and caring friends and loved ones to hold us up.

Prayer:

O God, our help in ages past, our hope for years to come, thank you for your support and strength. Thank you for the care and love of family and friends. With all this "support," we can bridge the valleys of life. In gratitude, we offer this prayer through Jesus Christ, our Lord and Savior. Amen.

SS2824

Bouquets That Are Loved

Prop: A bouquet of multicolored flowers

I brought some beautiful flowers with me. Look at all those colors! What different colors do you see? (Encourage the children to respond.)

God made the world and everything in it. God considers everything He made as "good," and He loves the things He created. In nature we see God's glory and majesty.

Boys and girls, people's faces are different colors, too: red, yellow, black, brown, and white. God loves all of them.

He loves all people, no matter where they live or what color of skin they have. "Jesus loves the little children, all the children of the world. Red and yellow, black and white, they are precious in his sight. Jesus loves the little children of the world." (If time permits, lead the children in singing this familiar song.)

The different colors of a bouquet of flowers and the many colors of people's skin–God loves all of them. They're all beautiful to Him.

Prayer:

Creator God, you must love color, for you put so much of it in the world you made and the human beings who were created in your image. We celebrate the richness of color, the beauty of your people, and the marvelous ways you made us different. Help us always to appreciate these differences, as well as the ways we are the same. We ask these things in Jesus' name. Amen.

SS2824

Pumping Us Up

Props: An inflated basketball (or some other inflated ball), a deflated ball, a needle air valve, and a hand pump

I have something which you will often see in a gymnasium or on a playground. What is this? (Display the inflated basketball.) How many of you have ever played with a basketball? (Encourage a show of hands.)

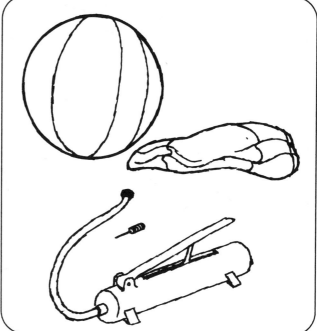

A lot of people enjoy playing basketball. They like to shoot the ball into the basket, and they like to bounce or dribble the ball on the floor. (Demonstrate by dribbling the ball.)

This ball will bounce like that because it has air inside it. The less air it has, the lower it will bounce. Let me show you. (Take the deflated basketball and try to dribble it.) This ball will not bounce at all; in fact, when I toss it down, it simply hits the floor and stays there.

This basketball won't bounce because it doesn't have any air in it. I don't think it would be much fun at all trying to play basketball with this ball.

Let's see if we can fix it. (Call on children to be helpers and pump up the deflated basketball with the needle air valve and hand pump.) There! The basketball is now filled with air. Let's see how it will bounce now. (Do so.) Ah, that's much better. This ball can bounce higher now because it has enough air inside it.

You and I are a little bit like these basketballs. Sometimes we are like the inflated basketball: we feel happy and "up"; we are filled with good thoughts and good feelings about ourselves. That's when we "bounce" along in life.

But sometimes we are like the deflated basketball: we feel sad and "down"; we are empty of good thoughts and good feelings about ourselves. We don't feel very "bouncy" and may feel that we want to "hit" the floor and stay there. Fortunately, when we feel like a deflated basketball, we are not alone. God is working hard to "pump us up," just as we pumped up the basketball that had little or no air inside. Through His Spirit, God makes us feel better about life and about ourselves.

God also works through the love of family and friends to "pump us up" and help us to feel like "bouncing" again.

When we feel "down," let's not give up, for God and our family and friends will help to "pump us up!"

But sometimes we are like a deflated basketball, one without any air in it: We feel sad and "down," we are empty of good thoughts and good feelings about ourselves. We are unable to "bounce" and may feel that we want to "hit" the floor and stay there.

Fortunately, when we seem like a deflated basketball, we are not alone. God is working hard to "pump us up," just as we pumped up the basketball that had little or no air inside. God's Spirit is helping to make us feel better, both about life and about ourselves.

God is also working through the love which others hold for us. Our family and our friends can also "pump us up" and help us to feel like "bouncing" again.

So when we feel "down," let's not give up. For God, family, and friends will help to "pump us up!"

Prayer:

> Father, Son, and Holy Spirit, we give you thanks that you are never far from from us. Because you love us and care about us, you are close at hand to help. Because you and family members and friends are around to "pump us up," we know that when we feel "down" it will be only for awhile. Thank you for working through your love and the love of others. We pray these things in Jesus' name. AMEN.

Playing the Game

Prop: A table or board game with a set of instructions or rules

How many of you like to play games? (Encourage a show of hands.) What games do you like to play? (Encourage the children to mention games.)

I have a game with me which you may recognize. It is a game I played when I was your age. It is called Monopoly™.

To play the game fairly, all people must follow the rules. Every game has a set of rules or directions telling how to play the game. Monopoly™ has a set, too. (Hold up the rules so that the children may see them.)

If a game ends early before there is a winner, it's usually because someone disobeyed the rules. Sometimes people want to win so badly, they do things that the rules don't allow. When someone decides to be unfair and take advantage of the other players, a game is no fun. Indeed, players may get angry because someone doesn't obey the rules.

Jesus said that the life of a Christian has a set of rules, too. These are directions which every Christian ought to obey: never repay evil for evil; share what you have; pray without making a big show of it; do not hurt others; be forgiving; do not lie; be kind; do not cheat; do not spread untrue stories about others.

Life is no fun unless people play according to the rules. People often become angry, and violence can result when others don't obey the rules.

Monopoly™ has a set of rules that come with it. Only by obeying those rules can the game be fun. The Christian life has a set of rules that come with it. Only by obeying Jesus' rules can life be fun for us.

Prayer:

>Creator God, maker of heaven and earth, thank you for all that you have made. Thank you especially for creating us in your image, with the capacity to think and love. Thank you also for giving us a set of rules by which to live. Help us to obey these rules, that our lives may be happy. These things we pray in Jesus' name. Amen.

Stopping Time

Prop: A stopwatch

I have something rather unusual with me. Do you know what this is? (Show the stopwatch to the children and invite their answers.) It's a kind of clock, somewhat like a watch. It is a stopwatch. It is used to measure the time of a race. It works like this. (Describe and illustrate the way the stopwatch works.)

When I push this button, the time begins to be measured, and when I touch this button, the time stops being measured. The number tells us how long the race took. (If time permits, you might time how long it takes the children to count to ten or how long it takes the children to do something else.) In a way, when I touch that second button, I stop time. All I have is the measured time for one of the races; no more time is added. The watch has stopped.

Sometimes we may feel we want to stop time. When we are really happy doing something, we would like that moment to last forever. When we have accomplished something that makes us feel good, we wish that feeling might never go away. When someone says something wonderful to us or about us, we wish that feeling would never end. When it's a beautiful day, and we feel "on top of the world," we want that feeling to stay with us always. Sometimes we want to stop time.

At other times, we would like to speed up time. When we are sick and want to get better, we wish the time would go quickly. When we are told that we can do things like help paint, bake cookies, have a pet, drive a car, or go out on a date when we "are older," then we want to grow up faster. We would like to speed up time.

SS2824

We cannot stop time, and we can't speed it up. We can ask God for a good memory when we want to slow down or stop time so we can remember the event, the moment, and the good feelings we had. We can celebrate each happy moment as it comes. Even though we realize that it will not last forever, we can remember it. We should ask God for patience when we want to speed up time, so we can be successful in taking each day as it comes.

Prayer:

God of the past, the present, and the future, you are the Lord of time. Sometimes we wish we were in control of time. Then we could stop it or slow it down if we wished; we could speed it up if we preferred. You alone are Lord of time. We ask you that we might have vivid memories, which will preserve the good times and good feelings we have. We ask you to give us patience that will help us deal with time that seems to move too slowly. We ask you in the name of Jesus Christ. Amen.

 SS2824

Opening Up

Props: A package of sweetened fruit-flavored drink mix, a pitcher of water, and a stirring spoon

I have a package of something which nearly everyone will recognize. What do I have in my hand? (Show the package of drink mix to the children.)This is a package of fruit-flavored drink mix. What flavor is your favorite? (Encourage the children to indicate their favorite flavors.)

I'm going to make some of this drink now. I have a pitcher full of water and a spoon. I will take the package of drink mix and put it into the water. (Put the unopened package of drink mix into the pitcher of water.) There! That will be delicious! (Take the spoon and begin stirring the water with the unopened package in it as children laugh and point out your mistake.)

What's the matter? Don't you think this is going to taste good? What's wrong? (Encourage the children to answer.) Oh, I see: I should have opened the package before I put it into the pitcher of water. (Do so, and then stir the mixture of powder and water.) There! That's better; now we have made some delicious fruit drink.

You and I are like that package of fruit-flavored drink mix. We are dropped into life when we are born, just as the fruit drink mix was put into the pitcher of water. Sometimes we stay to ourselves, thinking only of ourselves. In fact, we may be quite selfish. We are like that unopened package; we just float around not mixing with others as we should.

How much better it is when we open up and give of ourselves to others! When we love others, think about them, and do kind things for them, they do the same for us, and we know happiness. The Apostle Paul said we shouldn't do anything from selfishness or conceit, but in humility think others as better than ourselves. We shouldn't look only to our own interests, but also to the interests of other people (Philippians 2:3-4).

When we "open" ourselves and "mix" with others, we find that life is happier and more "delicious." Other people add to our joy, and we add to theirs.

Prayer:

Lord God, we give you thanks that you have chosen to relate to us and to be close to us. Thank you for getting "mixed up" with us. Most of all, we thank you for becoming one of us in Jesus Christ. These things we pray in His name. Amen.

SS2824

A Crutch

Prop: One of a pair of crutches

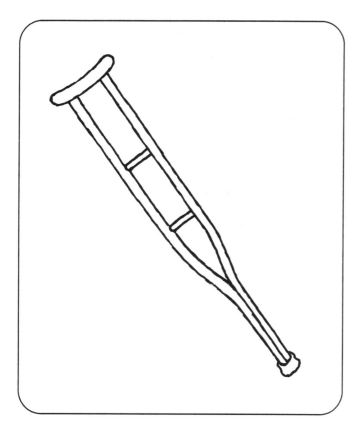

What do I have with me? (Encourage responses from the children.) It is a crutch. Have you ever seen someone use a crutch? (Again, encourage responses from the children.) Let me show you how a crutch works. (Demonstrate.)

A crutch helps a person who is hurt to get around. Without the crutch, that person would be unable to do the things many can do.

Sometimes the Holy Spirit acts as a crutch for us. He helps us when we feel down or tired, or when we feel we simply cannot do something.

The Holy Spirit is very important. Without the Spirit, we would not be able to do many things Christians should do.

When we really need Him, the Holy Spirit will help us to stand up and do what we need to do.

Prayer:

Gracious and helping God, we give you our thanks and our praise that you are always willing to help us "get back on our feet." Knowing that we can count on the Holy Spirit gives us confidence. We thank you in Jesus' name. Amen.

SS2824

Wired Together

Prop: A picture or drawing of telephone or electrical poles

I have a picture with me of electrical poles. How many poles are there in this picture? (Hold up the picture so children can count the poles.)

These poles appear to be separate from each other. One here, one there, one farther on. (Use the picture to illustrate by pointing.) *Distinct* and *detached* are two big words we could use to describe these poles. (Use hand gestures to illustrate visually *detached* and *distinct*).

But wait! If we look more closely and more carefully, we will see something interesting. Do you see something that connects the poles, something high up and very thin? What is that? (Encourage the children to respond.) There is a thin wire high up on the poles which connects them. The wire goes from one pole, to the next pole, to the next pole, to the next pole. (Trace the wire with your finger for the children.) The wire connects the poles on down the line as far as you can see. Sometimes there is a great distance between the poles that are connected.

Human beings are somewhat like electrical poles! You and I seem to be apart from each other. We appear to be separate, distinct, detached from one another. You're over there, and I'm over here. There is distance between us.

It would seem that "I am I" and "you are you," and that there is no connection between us. Yet, there is a connection: we are alive, and we are human beings, and God has made all of us in His image (Genesis 1:27). We are all special creations of God's handiwork.

God's love connects us. Even though we are all different from one another, God loves us, and His love is something we share with other people. God asks us to love one another as He loves us. We cannot love as perfectly as God does, but we can try. God will help us (empower us) to love others the best that we can. You and I (and all of us) are connected by the "wire of love." Through God's love for everyone, we are "wired together."

Prayer:

God, we thank you for creating us in your divine image, for loving us, and for asking us (and helping us) to love one another. You connect us and join us together. As "connected people," we want to love other people more fully. Fill us with your love, that it may overflow and "go down the line" to our neighbors. All these things we ask in the name of Jesus, who loved others fully and unconditionally. Amen.

Index